THREE SCORE Y

Three Score Years – and Then?

Reaching older people for Christ

RHENA TAYLOR

MONARCH
BOOKS

Mill Hill, London and Grand Rapids, Michigan

First published by Monarch Books in the UK in 2001,
Concorde House, Grenville Place,
Mill Hill, London, NW7 3SA.

Distributed by:
UK: STL, PO Box 300, Kingstown Broadway, Carlisle,
Cumbria CA3 0QS;
USA: Kregel Publications, PO Box 2607,
Grand Rapids, Michigan 49501.

ISBN 1 85424 521 X (UK)
ISBN 0 8254 6033 6 (USA)

British Library Cataloguing Data
A catalogue record for this book is available from the British
Library.

Book design and production for the publishers by
Bookprint Creative Services
P.O. Box 827, BN21 3YJ, England
Printed in Great Britain.

CONTENTS

ACKNOWLEDGEMENTS

The Outlook Trust was founded in 1992 as an interdenominational charity to inspire, resource, and encourage evangelism among older people in the UK.

Much of the information and many of the ideas in this book have been gained from being at the centre of this organization and knowing what different Outlook members are attempting for Christ across the country. Initially I intended naming the various members against the ideas and examples they were responsible for. However, this proved impossible. Instead I list below some to whose creativity and energy for Christ I know I am indebted but would also like to thank, at this point, all who responded to different pleas for help in putting this book together. To list them all would be impossible. The royalties from the book will go directly to the Outlook Trust.

Thank you: Peter Brierley of Christian Research (who provided so many of the facts referred to in this book), Edna Cleasby, Ruth Clinch, June Crome, Andrew Dyer, Ray and Phyl France, Walter and Mildred French, Mary

Glover, Leon and Elaine Greenhalgh, Joan Heybourn, Paul Gunstone, Peggy Hider, Stan and Nancy Hornsby, Grace Jacobs, Juanita Kirby, Jill Lawson, Ann Lear, Pam Marchant, Margaret Norrish, Cindy Proctor, Ray and Lily Read, Joyce Sefton, Sheila Shepheard, Ada Smith, Joy Tilley, Ron and Hazel Wilcox.

And finally: my two colleagues in the Outlook office, David Heydon and John Taylor, who had a lot to put up with during the writing of this book.

Rhena Taylor

PROLOGUE

Yesterday the telephone rang. A friend had heard I was writing this book. I recorded my responses.

FRIEND: ******************?!

ME: Don't argue. Why shouldn't I write a book on this? It's an important subject, especially today when the number of older people in the western world is increasing daily. Do you know that the number of people over pensionable age in the UK is projected to increase from over 10 million in 1998 to 12.2 million in 2021?[1]

FRIEND: *******************!

ME: No, the church is *not* "full of older people". According to Christian Research, in 1998, out of almost 8 million seniors in England, less than 1 million were attending church.[2] That's a potential harvest field of over 7 million people, which is growing as the population ages. They need reaching for Christ.

FRIEND: **!!!

ME: Yes, of course it's vital to preach the gospel to the
           young, and I know the "church of the future"
           depends on it. But there are many Christian pro-
           grammes and organizations across the country
           aimed at youth, and a mass of books to help the
           leaders of youth work. On the other hand, very
           few Christians are evangelizing older people.
           Why should they be left out?

FRIEND: ****

ME: Have they really "had their chance"? If you
           talked to as many older people as I do, you'd
           know how many have never heard and under-
           stood the gospel of Jesus. Anyway, there's
           another reason. Life's getting a lot harder for
           some of us. The faster the rate of change, the
           easier it is to be left behind. Life seems to have
           very little to offer the old today. It's only
           common sense to keep an eye on the future.

FRIEND: ****!!!

ME: OK. Your parents are better off than ever before
           and have just come back from their second
           "world tour". But recent figures show that nearly
           one third (32%) of all households in Great Britain
           consist of one person over pensionable age living
           alone,[3] with 18.7% of them living in what is rated
           as "poor housing"[4] and 22% living on less than
           half of the average income.[5] So we're possibly
           living longer, but life doesn't seem to offer that
           much to a lot of us.

FRIEND: ***?!

ME: Yes, I did say "we"! I'm "of pensionable age"
           these days. And if I didn't believe in Jesus I'd
           find life very different. We need Jesus, all of us;
           and the nearer we get to the end of life, the more
           we need to hear and understand what's really on
           offer from the Christian faith.

FRIEND: ************?

I know it might be difficult. That's what this book is all
about.

CHAPTER ONE
STARTING OUT

The first thing you need to deal with, when trying to explain to others that your mission in life is to preach the gospel to older people, is to get your terminology right!

This is not a small matter. No one likes admitting to being "old" these days, so what can we call our "target audience"? Is "older people" all right? If not: the elderly? Over 60's? Those in later life/years? Mature citizens? Retired people? The aged? Seniors? Senior citizens? Pensioners? Chronologically disadvantaged/advantaged? There seems no end to the efforts we make to get it right and I am only listing, as I'm sure you realize, the politer terms used.

Then there is the problem of what we call the fellowship/meeting/Bible study/special church service/lunch club that we want to start.

Just for your information, regarding the above: "Twinkling Lights in the Twilight Years", is definitely out, and "The Best is Yet to Be" suffers from over-kill. At the end of the chapter I have listed possible titles that I have come across, and must confess to a weakness for "KOBS" (Knocking on a Bit).

The problem of terminology is aggravated, of course, because we are talking of a possible age range of 40 years, and several generations. We cannot, when thinking of how to reach older people with the gospel, treat them as one audience. So I would ask you to think in terms of the "third age" and the "fourth age" and to define older people not by age, but by health and fitness. The "third age" are those "of pensionable age" who are mobile and on the whole are managing their daily lives without outside help, and the "fourth age" are those who need help in daily living. Perhaps they are in nursing or residential homes, or are housebound for one reason or another.

This is not in any way to see one group as more important than another. Nor should we make too much of this distinction or, necessarily, even mention it to the people involved. It is simply a means of making sure that we in the church have programmes (and evangelistic teams) suited to both groups. If you say "Why do it differently?" The answer is: Otherwise, in our ageist society, we might miss out one of those groups entirely.

After all, it is easy to lose sight of older people. Viewed from the outside today, the old have everything to lose and nothing to gain. Today's culture is centred on youth, and older people are only praised if they manage to look (and act) young for their age. The effort to sustain a false identity becomes a losing battle. Often people seem to be deliberately ignoring older people. It took me time to realize that was not the case. They simply do not see them.

Probably largely for these reasons, evangelism among the older generations has never been on the top line of the church agenda, if indeed it appears at all. So maybe we who are older Christians and recognize long life as a gift from God should find our vocation in reaching out with the message of the gospel to our peers at a time when they may be in great need. Remember how often it has been within the marginalized sections of society the greatest blessings have been seen.

Present church programmes

The church, over the years, has been fairly comfortable with the "fourth age" and does good work in that area. If I ask today what programmes a church has in place for older people, I am usually told that some of the congregation take services once a month in a local nursing home, that there is a fortnightly luncheon club or a monthly coffee morning, and – if they have given serious thought to the matter – that a pastoral team visits regularly. All of these are necessary and commendable, although I don't know that they are necessarily linked in people's minds with evangelism.

But, excellent though they are, these tend to major on the "fourth age". There is also the "third age", a generation set nearly to double in the next 25 years as the baby boomers of the '50s reach later years. Many of this generation are, and will be, more healthy, alert, and (in some cases) more financially secure than has ever been the case before. But by far the majority of these are not in church.

Those who are in the church are often well used, of course. They are the backbone of the church's catering committee, flower register, and church-cleaning team; but it is still a group of people the church is failing.

Courses to help us adjust to different life situations are offered today in the more active churches. I have seen many advertised for youth leaders, teenagers, job seekers, those planning marriage, new parents, and so on. If the church is more up-to-date, there might be one on retirement. But the one course missing in most churches today is the one that might affect a good part of their congregation: how to keep spiritually healthy and spiritually active during the 30 to 40 years that may follow retirement.

I try to keep in mind the comment of an older woman who had been a church member all her life. She spoke on her need for the church to help her re-adjust to her changing position in the community of the church, and to make sense of her ageing in the light of her faith. It was not that she felt her church was uncaring, nor that she was not loved there, but at this time of need, she felt their attention was elsewhere. I think that says it all: their attention was elsewhere.

No one is going to deny the need to call young people into the church of God. But then, no one does. There are, however, very few programmes designed to call unsaved older people into the church; people whose time might be considerably shorter. And one has to ask how welcome would they be when they got there? Is it true that the "church is full of old people"?

There is not much research done in this area, but in 1998 out of almost 8 million people in England aged 65 and over, less than 1 million attended church.[1] In 1994 Christian Research carried out a survey on church attendance which showed that only 1% of church goers start attending church when they are 60+, and of those whose church attendance started before they were 60, 42% stopped going between the ages of 60 and 64 and 38% stopped aged 65–74.[2]

One wonders why they stopped going. Perhaps some is fall-out caused by illness, lack of mobility or death. But I seem to have met many older people recently who have dropped out because "I somehow don't feel at home there any more".

Why do we need to see the over-60s as a separate group for evangelism? Because there are millions outside the Kingdom whom no one is targeting. Because it is not fun to grow old in today's society. Because the church has gone the way of the world in its attitude to older people: they are not of great interest. Because God is watching his own.

If we don't think about them and how to reach them, they will not be reached. If we don't want to reach them, they will not be reached.

The world calls it "the pensionable age", but I see the "young olds" with their own house, the family nearby, more money than they have had for some time, and holidays planned for some years ahead. But they have little interest in Christian things. I see lonely and frightened widows in their 80s or 90s whose pension is hardly sufficient to live on and who never signed a cheque before their husband's death. I see busy, cheerful "third-agers" who are quick to say, "I'm so busy I can't think how I ever had time to work", but still need Christ. I see red brick bungalows and net curtains behind which old people sit who never receive a visit except from the district nurse who checks on them briefly every fortnight. It is a wide and varied "target audience", but their needs are real and the door is open.

In ending this chapter, I include a short drama that could lead to a discussion with church leaders about evangelism to this age group. Whatever age we are, we either believe and accept Christ as our Saviour or we don't. Belief opens the door to glory. What refusal means I cannot tell.

Try this little skit on your church group, just to start them thinking.

THE "ONLY OLD"
by Rhena Taylor

Characters: A minister and an elderly lady.
Scene: Minister's study.

MINISTER   (*Trying not to look busy*) Well . . . Mrs . . . er . . .
           Watson, isn't it? You wanted to see me?
MRS G   It's Mrs Green, actually, . . . I expect you find
           all the names rather difficult.

MINISTER   Ah . . . yes . . . of course . . . Mrs Watson is the
           one that sits beside you in church. You ladies
           sometimes look all the . . . (*Realizes the trap he is
           walking into*) . . . er . . . all the . . .

MRS G   (*Pleasantly*) All the same, were you going to
           say, minister? Yes, I expect we do. We're much
           the same age group, you see.

MINISTER   (*Relieved*) Yes . . . and you all sit together . . . it's
           sometimes difficult . . . to . . . er . . . to . . . Well,
           now Mrs Wat . . . Green, I mean. What was it
           you wanted to see me about?

MRS G   I just wanted to share with you about some-
           thing new I think the Lord may be leading me
           and perhaps one or two others into.

MINISTER   Oh?

MRS G   It's about evangelism, leading people to
           Christ. There are so many people around here
           who never come to church, even at Christmas.
           We were thinking of visiting some of them.

MINISTER   Well, that's very good. I've been wanting to set
           up a pastoral team for some time . . . never got
           around to it somehow. I've been meaning to
           ask Tony Riggs to head it up. I'm sure he'd be
           good: children of his own, you see. Our
           Sunday School's really been dropping in
           numbers . . . and there're so many young fam-
           ilies around, dashing off to the supermarkets
           on Sundays now, I'm afraid. Yes, yes.
           Evangelism's very close to my heart, Mrs Wat
           . . . Green. I'm glad you've got the vision too.

MRS G   The thing is, my "vision", so to speak, is to concentrate on the elderly people in the district. There're a good many of them around too, living alone and often unhappy. I, . . . well, we, really – several of us are involved – would like to take the gospel to them.

MINISTER   (*Obviously turned off*) Well, yes, of course . . . but you're not thinking of evangelism *only* among the elderly, are you? I mean there're quite a lot of older people already in our congregation . . . can't have a church of only the old, you know. (*Laughs nervously*) Bad for the image really, isn't it?

MRS G   No. I think the church should be of all ages, of course. But there are so many programmes here already for the younger ones, and for families. We don't really make any effort to lead older people who never come to church to the Lord.

MINISTER   (*Defensive*) There's the lunch club.

MRS G   (*Patiently*) I know there's the lunch club. I run it. But we can only manage 20 at the most, and they are all church members. I'm talking about an evangelistic programme to reach others in the district who never come near us. Then there's the residential homes . . .

MINISTER   I go into Hanley House every month to take communion.

MRS G   You don't stay there long, minister. I was told you were out in just under fifteen minutes last week.

MINISTER   Mrs Green, I really don't have the time to do more. You know how it is . . .

MRS G   Yes, I do know how it is. That's why I want to make use of the people that *do* have a little more time: the older people in church. They can be encouraged to evangelize their own age group.

MINISTER   And fill the church with more old people?

MRS G   Would you rather have it three-quarters empty?

MINISTER   (*Flurried*) Yes. No. Of course I wouldn't. It's just . . . well . . . it isn't exactly a priority, is it, Mrs Green?

MRS G   Isn't it?

Possible titles for events and meetings with older people in mind

Seniors for Christ
Celebrate Age
A New Outlook
On Line with God
An Upside-Down World
Dreams and Visions
Stop the World: I Want to Get Off
Heavens Above!
World's Apart: or Are We?
Powering Up
Health and Healing
New Stones for New Giants

Riding High
Three Score Years and Then?
Heavens Above! Or Are They?
Outlook Towards Eternity
Steps to Eternity
Faith in the Future
Light in the Twilight Years
KOBS (Knocking on a Bit)

CHAPTER TWO

EVANGELISM IN ACTION

So evangelism among the over-60s is on your heart. Great. It's a very large and increasing field and could do with more enthusiasts. I think it was the evangelist J John, using the story of David and Goliath, who commented that there are two ways of facing a big challenge in life. You can say, "It's so big, I'm going to run away" or you can say, "It's so big. I can hardly miss." The latter is surely true with 10 million plus older people around somewhere.

It is really not surprising that one of the things we are learning less about (or forgetting fast) as the decades pass is how to communicate comfortably face to face. It has, of course, always been possible to visit a Christian church and leave without exchanging a word with anyone, but now we can do the same in the post office, the bank, the shops and supermarkets, the doctor's surgery, the book sale in the village and the bus or train. Recently I chatted for some minutes with an older person in a post office queue. I think we were discussing a problem with her television. When she had been served and turned to go, she said to me, "Thank you for talking to me." I looked after her, incredibly sad. Was she so lonely that a brief chat with a stranger was so special?

Even if we are still working in later years, the world of work requires less and less that we talk to each other. Even the telephone lines fall silent as soon as we and our business colleagues start communicating by e-mail.

And yet most of us know in our hearts that the things that matter to us, that help us to be people and enjoy life, most often come from human beings close to us: things like talking, laughing, crying, giving someone a hug, forming friendships inside and outside the family. Relationships are really what life is all about: getting to know people, what they think, what they want; and finding out, as we go, how to break through the perhaps closed door of vague spirituality to introduce someone to the glory of the Godhead.

As evangelists, older people do not have too many advantages but probably in this matter we do. Sharing stories of hip replacements in the doctor's surgery, chatting on a park bench on a summer day, sharing fury at the bus which never gets there on time, discussing the latest development in our favourite "soap". Relationships can be made. The field is there. Now for the harvest.

So what do we need to begin?

(1) *A call from God.* By this I mean serious work in this area, not the natural talking and witnessing to friends and

neighbours who may be in this age group. To seek to take the gospel of Christ to older people can be an unattractive mission field in our ageist society. There is little glamour attached (you won't easily grab the headlines in the Christian press) and possibly little recognition by your church. So check it out. Is this truly God's call to you?

(2) *A clarity of message.* As we share the gospel with older people we need to be clear and ready with what we want to say, and open to God's help and leading to help us make this message real to the person in front of us. Some people may have gone to church for 40 years or more and never been challenged by the true message of Christ. That message is blurred in our modern world, and the way we live our lives distracts from the truth. We need to make the message clear.

(3) *A recognition that this is war*! When sharing the gospel of Christ with an unbeliever, the enemy is the same, whoever the person may be. Opposition can and will come almost immediately in various ways. You will need to fight your way onto this particular platform, using the armour suggested by the apostle Paul in Ephesians 6: truth and integrity, clean living, readiness to share the gospel, faith that does not waver, courage and the word of God.

(4) *An excitement about the message we have to deliver.* Today's society can accept the principle, "If it works, go for it", so let us make sure that, for us, our life as a

Christian, our trust in God, and our love for Jesus "works". That is the most powerful testimony we can offer, and it's catching. So often today, we older people are made to feel out-dated and "past it" because of our inability to keep up with the information revolution taking place on this tiny planet, earth. But if the connection all Christians can have with the Creator God is real to us, and if we are truly conscious that we are communicating with powers far greater than any on earth and greater far than any single thing humanity can offer, then we have a message that will be heard.

(5) *Others with the same vision*. God does not really mean us to tackle this alone. I do know some older Christians who witness faithfully alone because they don't have the choice. One lived in a sheltered housing complex and regularly ran coffee mornings where she got to know her neighbours. At Christmas they sang carols together and talked about the words. Gradually the coffee morning became a little "seekers" group and then a Bible study. Another older Christian ordered some copies of *Challenge* newspaper and distributed it to the people she knew in the collection of apartments where she lived, later calling to see if they would like to order it. A number did. We can sometimes be called upon to witness alone for a time, but even the disciples went out in pairs. Pray that God will give you others who are like-minded.

Let's assume you have a small group and you are "ready to go".

What next?

Without being too negative on this subject, I'll tell you what often happens next, possibly because often would-be evangelists to the elderly are elderly themselves. We get together, sell the idea to our church, and start working on a strategy of approach to the unchurched elderly, only to find Muriel has slipped on the stairs and broken her ankle, Alice is being unexpectedly re-housed some distance away and Jim has suspected prostate cancer. Take it in your stride. It's only beginning. Get the prayer-backing organized and make plans.

It may be wise first to put in place some kind of training. For example:

(a) Find out whether your team are able to explain what a Christian is. Help them to talk about their faith within the group. Check whether they are truly convinced of the truth of the gospel.

(b) Help them share their testimonies of failure and success of their Christian life within the group and to get used to the idea that they can talk about their Christian life without making it sound trouble-free. (Many will never have been asked to share their experiences of the Lord.)

(c) Consciously care for their spiritual growth and their knowledge of the Bible. Make a real effort to help one another learn and repeat biblical texts. Carry cards in your pockets!

(d) Help them to understand the needs of older people

outside the church who have no real faith. Try some "role play" to show how we can talk to others about the Lord.

If you are serious about this and willing to attempt a little "street evangelism", you can try out a simple exercise. I have introduced a number of small groups of older people to what I call my "point system".

First steps in "street evangelism"

The idea is that three or four Christians, preferably in the age group we are discussing, get together in prayer on, say, a Saturday morning, near a shopping centre. They then separate for a couple of hours and just look for opportunities to chat to older people they meet: in a queue, on a bench, in a coffee shop. Then they keep a small private record. If they get "church" into the conversation they get one point; if they get "God" in, they get two; if they get "Jesus" in, they get three, and if they give away the tract they have in their hand, they get four. Then they come back and share what has happened.

This is meant to be light-hearted but also prayerful and serious. Coming back together, we can be honest about what opportunities the Lord did or did not give us. We remember it is his work. Some may not have got the chance to speak. Others scored high or low, but the important thing is they tried. And that makes you and them feel just great! I remember a little lady (who must have been over 80) saying, beaming, to her minister on Sunday: "I got some points yesterday, Vicar!"

What does this exercise do? It helps us realize we can be a witness for Christ, and gives us a sense of joy in doing it. Of course there are Christians doing this naturally and often. This exercise is for the rest of us. Let us, however, just get a taste for it, and maybe it won't be so difficult the next time. Remember, the Lord gives the opportunities. All we do is take the ones he offers us. However, if we consistently fail to respond to given opportunities, then we might receive fewer. This book offers many ways of reaching older people for Christ. But we need the courage to open our mouths and speak, and also the ability to use the Bible.

I am one of those people for whom, every time I feel there is an opportunity to share my faith with someone, every Bible verse I ever knew disappears out the window. So I'd like to share with you my Biblical "PIN" (Personal Identification Number): 1135. It is 1 Peter 1.3–5. My notes below are in italics.

Praise be to the God and Father of our Lord Jesus Christ.
(Any god will not do)
In his great mercy
(Motivated by compassion and love)
He has given us new birth into a living hope through the resurrection of Jesus Christ from the dead . . .
(Christ died on the cross but rose again, so showing himself a conqueror over sin and death, and invites us to share that victory)
. . . into an inheritance that can neither perish, spoil, or fade – kept in heaven for you who through faith are shielded by God's power . . .

> *(Heaven awaits, and in the meantime if we are steady in faith, God is watching over us – try 1 John 5.4–5 on that one)*
>
> . . . until the coming of salvation that is ready to be revealed in the last time.
>
> *(And there is salvation and joy ahead.)*

You could always choose this PIN for your bank account: 1135. 1 Peter 1.3–5! It really is useful when unexpected opportunities arise.

Remember always that the words of the Bible come from God. They are infinitely more powerful than ones we make up for ourselves. One way of offering ourselves to God for this kind of unrehearsed evangelism is to learn some special verses, perhaps ones that helped you make a decision for Christ. Pray, "Please Lord give me the opportunity to share this verse with someone today." Then go for a walk, and see what happens.

Frequent responses

Let us now think about some of the most frequent responses we hear from older people when we try to reach them with the gospel.

A very common one is: "But I'm a Christian already, aren't I?"

Well: aren't they?

Finding that out – if we ever do – is not easy and perhaps not even necessary. Religion to some older people is a private matter, not to be easily discussed. We need to find a gentle way to pursue the conversation. We are all individuals and the Holy Spirit will lead us. But here are some areas, especially, though not entirely, with the "fourth age" in mind, through which we may seek to enter someone's more private life.

Rejection is something some seniors feel if they are separated from spouse and family through death or institutionalization. They can experience a feeling of being "put on the shelf", forsaken or cast off. The Christian holds the message that God has not forsaken them. Matthew 28.20 *... and surely I am with you always, to the very end of the age.*

Forgiveness is a lovely word. Which of us reaches later years and bears no hurtful memories? Perhaps we are still cherishing bitter and angry thoughts about someone else? Perhaps there is a sin in our own life that we have never confessed to anyone and we feel a strong need to "put things right". Whether we need forgiveness or we need to offer it to others, there is healing surrounding the word "forgiveness". Can we lead someone to peace in the blood of Christ that cleanses from all sin? 1 John 1.7 *But if we walk in the light, as he is in the light, we have fellowship with one another, and the blood of Jesus, his Son, purifies us from all sin.*

Assurance of heaven is another door into which we can fit a key. Death, after all, is approaching as the years pass. Our society doesn't approve now of hell-fire preaching, but we can turn the key the other way. The death of a Christian is the beginning of life. John 5.24 *I tell you the truth. Whoever hears my word and believes him who sent me has eternal life and will not be condemned. He has crossed over from death to life.*

Fear is sometimes an unexpressed lock which we can touch gently, like a doctor running his expert hands over some part of the body, seeking to find the source of the pain. "What are you afraid of? Everyone is afraid sometimes . . ." 1 Peter 5.7 *Cast all your anxiety upon him because he cares for you.*

Healing of bodily pain can be another. I have heard of Christians just gently laying their hands on some part of another's body and praying. Sometimes pain lessens and even goes. So many pains in our bodies come from anxiety and worry. John 14.27 (the "legacy" of Jesus) *Peace I leave with you; my peace I give to you . . . Do not let your hearts be troubled and do not be afraid.*

Prayer is rarely refused. It's as if some people don't feel they know how to pray and they want someone to do it for them. When we pray they can feel that God is there, and the very awareness of the belief of another can cause them to open that door just a little wider. Luke 11.9–10 *Ask and it will be given to you; seek and you will find; knock and the door will be opened . . . for everyone who asks receives; he who seeks finds; and to him who knocks, the door will be opened.*

Of course, there may still be objections. For 40 or 50 years your new friend has said the same things to "church people": "God can't be a God of love with all this suffering around"; "The Bible's full of contradictions. It can't be true"; "I really don't have the time for church." But something, somewhere (bereavement?

illness? grandchildren? losing their home? retiring from work?) can get the wheels moving again. We need to go on looking, hoping, praying. God is on our side.

Unexpected things can happen that often have nothing at all to do with us. An older woman confined to a wheel-chair who loves to sit looking out of a particular window where trees grow by a river, sees a vision of Jesus. An older man has what would seem to be a miraculous answer to prayer and is tumbling over himself to tell you all about it. Suddenly someone who has been consistently hostile changes overnight.

I have often felt with really old people that God is very near. They do not have to reach far up to him. He who taught us compassion and love is there ready to take them into his kingdom. "Even to your old age and grey hairs I am he. I have made you and I will carry you." (Isaiah 46.4) I wonder how old the woman with the issue of blood was? We read about her in Matthew 9.21. She didn't do much (just touched the hem of his garment) for the Lord to say, "Your faith has saved you." And it made a huge difference.

So, how about the "young-olds", the "third agers"? Where can they be found? Are there "strategies" we need to put in place to reach them?

Third agers are all around us, but sometimes we fail to notice them because they often look just like us. We expect them to live in small houses or flats and live quiet lives, when in fact they are often still in the homes they had before, busier than they ever were when at work, and often open to doing something quite new and challenging.

We may find them on holiday in different resorts both at home and abroad; they are at shopping malls and sports centres, running literacy programmes in Botswana, behind the counter in charity shops, sitting on the District Council Committee, at health farms and hospitals, enjoying rambling clubs, behind the Mothers' Union cake stall. You may even find seniors with spiritual needs sitting in the pews of your own church.

Once you find third agers, you will need time to establish relationships with them. Many will feel they've been around long enough to know their own minds and do not really want to make a major change in the way they live and think. So many people are pressing opinions on them, and the least sense of being "pushed" will often bring resistance.

So we need to take our time and establish a friendly relationship which they feel will continue whether or not they accept what we are saying. If we ourselves are in this age group, this is not too difficult. We can join in the activities above. Then the testimony of our lives will be the most important part of our armour and often lead to the questions which we are waiting to hear. More than one person in this age group has become a Christian and asked "Why did no one tell me about this sooner?" Why, indeed?

Many third agers are becoming Christians today because someone has invited them to a home Bible study or a discussion group. They feel welcome there because there is usually a friendly and caring atmosphere and freedom for people to express their opinions. Questions (not always answered glibly) are encouraged.

Once they have found the Lord, they can become the best evangelists of all.

CHAPTER THREE

THE BIBLE AND OLD AGE

One of the most important aspects of Christian ministry with older people is for us to examine our own attitudes to old age in the 21st century. We need to confront our own prejudices and fears, and become confident of Christ's victory won for us over fear and death. When we are accustomed to fighting our own battles and winning more than we lose, then we can help others.

Let us think through the meaning of old age for our generation and try to understand from the word of God and the experiences he leads us through, how we can witness to Jesus Christ during old age.

So what does the Bible teach about old age?

Are we supposed to enjoy old age?

In Israelite society to live to old age was to be desired, a blessing from God, a crown of splendour. The Bible assumes we will be glad to live for a long time.

Grey hair is a crown of spendour; it is attained by a

righteous life.

Proverbs 16.31

Grey hair is the splendour of the old.

Prov. 20.29

Children's children are a crown to the aged and parents are the pride of their children.

Prov. 17.6 (Think that one out!)

Honour your father and mother so that you may live long in the land the Lord your God is giving you.

Exodus 20.12, repeated Ephesians 6.2

Keep my commands in your heart for they will prolong your life many years . . .

Prov. 3.2, 3.16, 4.10, 9.11

We don't, of course, know what it meant to "live long" in Old Testament times. For all we know, the expectation of life in those days could have been the 30s. However, although we often hear today "I hope I don't live as long as that!" we don't really know if we mean it. Self-preservation is said to be the strongest natural instinct in mankind and, in any case, we are not really going to have the choice. We will slip out of life as unconsciously as we once entered it, when the Lord intends it to happen.

Perhaps all we can say about this now is that God is sovereign and in control. He is not making a mistake about the time he calls us "home". If he lets us live on, he does so because there is work for us to do. Perhaps the very gifts and qualities of an older person (which we look into as we go through this chapter) are what is needed to keep our society steady today, at a time when the Christian faith and morality are being challenged on every side.

Remember, the Holy Spirit does not work through you only until you are 60. Joy and delight is not the prerogative of the young. Nor are visions and dreams of what new things God may be calling us to. Noah was certainly a "good old age" when he supervised the building of the Ark (Genesis 7.6). John was in his nineties when he was given the visions that led to the writing of Revelation. The only difference inside us may be that we are becoming aware that the evening is falling. We are getting a little nearer home. But what's wrong with that? Do we really want a day without the evening? And doesn't "home" have a comforting feel about it?

Be confident. Maybe in our culture, grey hair cannot always be seen as the splendour of the old as Proverbs 20.29 says. But the thought is right. The evening light can fall upon us. We will have more time to spend in his presence. The Bible can be read more carefully, perhaps more alone. Prayer can cover those we love wherever they may be. Those older people who draw close to the Lord in this way rather than forcing themselves to keep busy, show his splendour in their eyes. Nearly all of us know such people.

We can enjoy the homeward journey. If we have no family near, we can take to ourselves the young and the old that are near us as our friends, and love and pray for them. However long we live, our years here are "but fleeting in his sight". Let us take them as a gift from God.

So here is our first mission statement: *I believe old age is a blessing from God.*

Should older people expect to be respected?

It is clear from the Old Testament that in Israelite society the aged were expected to demonstrate wisdom and so were revered. The Mosaic law contains the words, "Rise in the presence of the aged, show respect for the elderly and revere your God" (Leviticus 19.32). In the biblical "history books" (2 Chronicles 10.6–15 for example) when the young took over from the old, it seems confusion follows. In the New Testament respect for the old is also seen in Paul's instruction to Timothy: "Do not rebuke an older man harshly but exhort him as if he were your father . . ." 1 Timothy 5.1.

However, it is clear in the Bible that the old were not wise by virtue of being old. They were wise because they had followed and obeyed the Lord for many years. When that is the case in our Christian family, then the young will listen and look. The old must be worthy of respect before it is given.

After all, it isn't just respect for the old that has disappeared in today's society. It is – in many cases – respect for anything or anyone. Nothing is sacred. There is no fear of God and people use his name carelessly, without thinking anything of it. It is their loss. The sense of respect is often a greater benefit to the giver than the receiver.

Here is our second mission statement: *Older people have to earn respect as do others.*

Can we really pass on the faith to the next generation?

It is clear from Scripture that older people are seen to be those who pass on the faith to those who follow them. They are the teachers to the next generation. The Psalmist writes,

Even when I am old and grey, do not forsake me, O God, till I declare your power to the next generation, your might to all who are to come.

Psalm 71.18

... what we have heard and known, what our fathers have told us. We will not hide them from their children; we will tell the next generation the praiseworthy deeds of the Lord, his power, and the wonders he has done.

Psalm 78.3–4

One generation will commend your works to another; they will tell of your mighty acts. They will speak of the glorious splendour of your majesty . . . They will celebrate your abundant goodness and joyfully sing of your righteousness.

Psalm 145.4–7

We might be tempted to think, "Some hope in today's society!"

So how can we "declare our faith to the generations following"? Concentrate on the family? Continue to teach in the much-diminished Sunday School?

If we are going to be of use to the generations coming up behind us, we have to turn towards them. It doesn't work the other way. The world of information processing and hypertext is available to us, as to others, but perhaps we feel much of that is beyond us. However, there are other ways to witness to the power of Jesus. I recall a quotation attributed to St Francis of Assisi: "Go out into all the world and preach the gospel. Use words if you have to." If we don't use words, what do we do? Can we use the following?

Attitudes: How much at peace are we with our bodies? How content with our physical condition? How welcoming to others? How willing to get close to them and listen? How relaxed and free of strain are we? I have often heard a younger person say of a senior, "I know she didn't want to go to that residential home but somehow now she looks so peaceful about it."

Time: How do we use it? Are we allowing time for God to speak to us? Are we available to others?

Space: How about sitting somewhere else in church so you get to know others? Try another service now and again, so you don't insist that the way you like to worship is best. You could meet a few younger generations that way. Have you ever let younger people use your home to meet in? Are you reluctant to go and speak to young people at the church coffee time because the older people are always expected to sit at the same table? Perhaps to ask them how things are going in their new job?

Writing: How about letters? To lonely students in their first year? To the grandchildren on their birthdays? Could you keep an eye on the local papers and see if sometimes you can appear in the "Letters" column if there is an opportunity for a Christian point of view? Have you been offended about something on the television? Write and protest. Stand up for what you believe. It's important.

Music: How about asking for help to learn some of the more modern hymns? Get the hang of the "top ten" and comment on the words people are singing. Support and encourage the music group at church. Be interested.

There are more ways of declaring the power of God than speaking it!

Here is our third mission statement: *I'm going to do my part with those younger than I am.*

Do I really believe myself to be a valid and useful part of the Body of Christ?

The very fact that there is relatively little about old age in the Bible suggests that God does not see old people as being in a special category. The church is the body of Christ and the body of Christ is the people in the church: all of them. The promises of God include the old.

> . . . You are no longer foreigners and aliens, but fellow citizens with God's people and members of God's household . . .
>
> Ephesians 2.19

> There is neither Jew nor Greek, slave nor free, male nor female, [Young nor old?] for you are all one in Christ Jesus.
>
> Galatians 3.28

> And afterward, I will pour out my spirit on all people; your sons and daughters will prophesy; your old men will dream dreams, your young men will see visions.
>
> Joel 2.28

[Praise Him] kings of the earth and all nations, you princes and all rulers on earth, young men and maidens, old men and children.

Psalm 148.11–12

Here is the fourth mission statement: *I believe I have a rightful place in the Body of Christ.*

How can I keep growing in Christ?

If we stop growing as Christians, we will be in danger of becoming spiritually weak which may allow fear to take over if things go wrong suddenly. The Bible reminds us of this:

Therefore we do not lose heart. Though outwardly we are wasting away, yet inwardly we are being renewed day by day . . . we fix our eyes not on what is seen, but on what is unseen. For what is seen is temporary, but what is unseen is eternal.

2 Corinthians 4.16 & 18

The path of the righteous is like the first gleam of dawn, shining ever brighter till the full light of day.

Proverbs 4.18

Those that are planted in the house of the Lord, they will flourish in the courts of our God. They will still bear fruit in old age; they will stay fresh and green, proclaiming, "The Lord is upright; he is my Rock, and there is no wickedness in him."

Psalm 92.13–15

The new is not behind us. It is ahead of us no matter how old we are. We must be careful not to let "oldness" take over our lives. We must grow and make progress. Our bodies may be falling apart, but our spirit can be renewed day by day. Let us not age in a way that makes us become old spiritually. Let newness grow in us.

St Augustine (354–430 AD)

So how do we stay "fresh and green"? Some suggestions:

(1) "Great peace have they who love your law, and nothing can make them stumble" (Psalm 119.165). Read and study the Bible. If it is an "old friend" and falling apart, try a modern version. Sometimes seeing the same text in different words gives us fresh insight. Try learning them. Carry a card in your pocket with one or two of them on it. Isaiah 55.11 gives us the promises that the word of God will not return to him empty. "It will not return to me empty, and will accomplish what I desire and achieve the purpose for which I sent it."

(2) Keep your prayer life going. Perhaps have a special place in the house for it. Light a candle, put an open Bible there, have a text card up, anything that marks it as a special place where you meet with God. Guard your prayer time carefully. There is no short cut to spiritual maturity. This is a college we do not graduate from.

(3) Go to a church, and don't forget the coffee time. If the sermons all seem directed at young families and tell you things you know already, then find other ways of being fed – books, tapes, Christian newspapers or magazines. Borrow old copies from someone who you know

has them. They are usually only too glad to pass them on. Keep your mind alert and have some interest in the general Christian scene. Feed yourself with Christian thinking (books, newspapers. . .). Take an interest in things beyond yourself so that your mind does not circle around your own situation too much.

(4) Make sure you have some Christian fellowship in the week. Join (or host) a housegroup/ a discussion group/ a "seekers" group/ a "Wednesday Afternoon Fellowship", and learn in it. It is important to be with other Christians. They need you as much as you need them (Hebrews 10.24–25). Let us consider how we may spur one another on towards love and good deeds. Let us encourage one another – and all the more as we see the Day approaching.

(5) Make sure you are giving generously. I liked an observation I heard recently. "Have you ever noticed how small a pound coin looks in the supermarket and how big in church?" You might take up the cause of a Christian charity and link up with a missionary society which always needs support. If you start feeling anxious about money it's a sign to increase your giving. Try it. It works. Tithe carefully. If we give to God, we are never the losers.

Here is the fifth mission statement: *I believe in spiritual growth!*

And in the darkness, hang on!

The reality of the pain and failing strength of old age is described in vivid metaphors in the Bible:

Remember your Creator in the days of your youth, before the days of trouble come and the years approach when you will say, "I find no pleasure in them" . . . Remember him – before the silver cord is severed, or the golden bowl is broken; before the pitcher is shattered at the spring, or the wheel broken at the well . . .

Ecclesiastes 12.1 & 6

The length of our days is seventy years – or eighty if we have the strength; yet their span is but trouble and sorrow, for they quickly pass and we fly away.

Psalm 90.10

Even to your old age and grey hairs I am he. I am he who will sustain you. I have made you and I will carry you; I will sustain you and I will rescue you.

Isaiah 46.4

Do not cast me away when I am old; do not forsake me when my strength is gone . . .

Psalm 71.9

Even in darkness light dawns for the upright, for the gracious and compassionate and righteous man.

Psalm 112.4

Why is light given to those in misery and life to the bitter of soul, to those who long for death that does not come?

Job 3.20–21

Because he loves me, says the Lord, I will be with him in trouble, I will deliver him and honour him. With long life will I satisfy him and show him my salvation . . .

Psalm 91.14

And Jacob said to Pharaoh, "The years of my pilgrimage are 130. My years have been few and difficult and they do not equal the years of the pilgrimage of my fathers . . ."

Genesis 47.9

Let him who walks in the dark, who has no light, trust in the name of the Lord.

Isaiah 50.10

He has made my skin and my flesh grow old . . . surrounded me with bitterness and hardship. He has made me dwell in darkness like those long dead.

Lamentations 3.4–6

. . . His compassions never fail. They are new every morning. Great is your faithfulness . . .

Lamentations 3.22–23

Here is the sixth mission statement: *I believe that God is with me at all times and in all circumstances.*

The very approach of death can be a special time of witness

This is a letter written by a friend, a doctor and an early member of Outlook, who knows her death at 65 from cancer is near:

I am aware that I will be moving on soon, into a different life. Am I sad? No. I have a feeling something is almost completed. But not sad. My husband and family will be sad. I hope they will remember me – often, but they must make what they can of their lives. The seasons will go on changing. I have watched them 65 times. It's their turn now.

Although I tire too easily to do many of the things I'd like to, I have to do and enjoy what I can. I'll not welcome the end but I know it's there and may be quite sudden.

I am conscious of the love and presence of Jesus, and know that he will take my hand to lead me safely home. People and incidents from my past come into my mind frequently – but I don't feel near to them, or heaven.

I think what I am trying to say is that, at the end, our ties to our Lord should be stronger than those to earthly friends and concerns.

Love, Joan.

(*Joan Pearson, Cambridge, UK December 2000*)

Now we know that if the earthly tent we live in is destroyed, we have a building from God, an eternal house in heaven, not built by human hands.

2 Corinthians 5.1

It does not mean the struggles are necessarily over. I cherish another letter written to me by a former professor who really knew the Lord, Donald Denman. He was close to his death and wrote as follows: "The 'good fight' is still to be fought at 89; the last lap of the race 'looking unto Jesus' is no less vigorous than all the others!"

A healthy reminder again that we do not graduate until we reach heaven.

Here is the seventh mission statement: *I believe that death is the gateway to heaven*.

We are not dismayed at the approach of old age because he who has walked with us through life is not going to leave us now. Let us refuse the fears of a society in a crisis of faith, with men "faint from terror, apprehensive of what is coming on the world" (Luke 21.26) and play our part with courage as ambassadors for Christ in this new century.

CHAPTER FOUR

THE CHURCH AND ITS OLDER MEMBERS

A fact to remember: As young people are not the church of tomorrow, neither are older people the church of yesterday.

How can the church care spiritually for the older people within it?

In chapter 1 I mentioned an 80-year-old woman, an active church member all her life, who commented on her need for the church to help her re-adjust to her changing position in the community of the church and to make sense of her ageing in the light of her faith. It was not that she felt her church was uncaring, nor that she was not loved there, but at this time of her need, she felt their attention was elsewhere.

Think about those words. At this "time of her need", she felt "their attention was elsewhere". It is a fact. Many church leaders today are not really interested in the spiritual needs of the older churchgoer.

This is a serious matter in the light of the growth of the ageing population and the increasingly difficult situations many older people find themselves in. Are we supposed to look after our own spiritual growth at a time in our lives in which we are likely to see more testing and change and fear than at any other time?

How can we help those older people already in the church to keep growing in their knowledge of the word of God and the love of the Lord Jesus?

Let us consider the situations some of them could be in. All characters described below are entirely fictional.

Geoffrey

The Situation. Geoffrey has been a member of the Parochial Church Council in the church for a very long time. He is now in his late 70s. At the moment he is the church treasurer and one of the district wardens. The young minister who has recently arrived finds him very difficult to deal with indeed. He seems to block everything suggested to him with the attitude, "You don't understand this church like I do", and goes his own way despite suggestions for change. Clearly he feels that his work in the church is now the only thing that gives him an identity.

Suggested response. We need to ask ourselves: How much interest has been shown in Geoffrey's spiritual growth over the years since his retirement from the business he worked for? What encouragement has been given him to grow in Christ and find in later years new fields of joy and service while others take on the leadership of the church?

What can be done for Geoffrey? The suggestions that follow may or may not "work" for individuals, but they are based – as is all this book – on what has been gen-uinely attempted:

Geoffrey basically needs a change of scene and thought. He is an intelligent and hard-working man. Could his mind be turned on other matters than holding onto the church administrative tasks he has carried out for the last 20 years? The UK is a little more familiar now with older people going to college (something done in the USA for a long time). Are there theological courses or a correspon-dence course he could be encouraged to enter? Is there some qualification he could seek? Is he aware of Christian organizations, including missionary societies, that are looking for short-term service from older people?[1] When we grow in the Spirit and learn more about the Bible, somehow we hear God's voice more plainly and other ministries seem "just to arrive".

Or there is quite possibly other work he could do within the church. If he has a heart for others, he could form (or join) something like a Care Team in the church. His contribution could well be to help the older church members (and other local senior citizens) to manage their finances and fill in the mass of forms they are expected to deal with today. Could he offer some help to those strug-gling to become computer literate? Could he, in other words, become more people-literate and less committee-literate? Perhaps a church library is needed (one of the most neglected opportunities within churches) and he could start that off and recommend books, tapes or CDs in the services. Is there a pastoral visiting team he could join, specially to visit men on their own? If there isn't, could he offer such visits through the church to the social services?

You can see the direction of this. Yes, Geoffrey will cease to be "The Church Treasurer", thus making room for someone else. He might, however, become a much happier and more fulfilled person.

Gladys

The Situation. Gladys, in her early 80s, has been coming to church all her life, but since she gave up the young people's work, she has not felt needed in the actual ministry of the church and is sinking silently into being one of the "little grey ladies at the back of the church". She is always there but sees church as part of her way of life, rather than the body of Christ of which she is a part. But 1 Corinthians 12.14–15 reminds us, "The body is not made up of one part but of many. If the foot should say, 'Because I am not a hand I do not belong to the body', it would not for that reason cease to be part of the body . . .'"

What should we do about Gladys?

Suggested Response. First, we could take an interest in knowing where she is, spiritually, and look for ways in which she could increase in her knowledge of God's word and grow in the Lord. Check if she is part of a housegroup or a small group of some sort. When do your housegroups (if you have them) meet? In the evening and possibly some distance away from where Gladys lives? Perhaps the first thing is to see that a small group is in place on a weekday afternoon (or morning) and that Gladys is gently urged into one. I recognize that people often feel that housegroups should be a mixture of people so that older people are not isolated, but be practical. Coming out in the evening is just not possible for some older people, especially in the winter.

Next (like all of us) Gladys needs teaching, and some of that can be done by the church leaders as well as in a small group. When was a sermon last given to the early morning service (where at least three-quarters of the congregation are over 60) on the spiritual challenges of later years? What picture or warning of the temptations that come with age and how to overcome them in the Lord? What challenge towards a courageous witness in old age? Why should she have to work it all out for herself?

Finally, Gladys needs to be needed (as we all do). Not every "tea and coffee type job" has to be done by the brisk and efficient 50+s, and there could be other tasks about the church she could become involved in if someone really thought about it. Consciously seek them. Are there special people she could pray for? Someone she could visit who needs company? How about helping with the "mums and tots" sometimes? We are the body of Christ. Everyone matters.

Arthur

The Situation. I have to mention Arthur because, in fact, he isn't there at all. He hasn't been able to get to church for over six months because of an arthritic hip which makes it impossible for him to go further than the village shop. He's not even on the waiting list yet, and the hospital tells him that perhaps the year after next . . . At first, everyone was very caring. They took him tapes of the sermon and occasionally someone would bring him by car. But then the person with the car left the area and, it must be admitted, Arthur lived a fair distance from church, and so somehow it just stopped and he passed out of mind.

Suggested Response. Try not to forget the "Arthurs". They need us and are part of our fellowship. Do you have a pastoral visiting team in place? If not, at least try to keep the contact going and see him still as a member of the church. He could be asked and brought to special events and share in prayer needs and so on. " 'For I was hungry and you gave me something to eat; I was thirsty and you gave me something to drink, I was a stranger and you invited me in, I needed clothes and you clothed me, I was sick and you looked after me' . . . and the King said . . . 'whatever you did for one of the least of these brothers of mine, you did for me'" (Matthew 25.35–36, 40). Maybe the need isn't water, or clothes, or medicine. Maybe it is only kindness.

Annie

The Situation. Annie is something of a pain. She is a long-standing member of the church and is now in her late 70s. She is one long complaint. The services aren't as they used to be. The music is so loud her ears hurt. She can't see the words on the acetates and has never really taken in that there is a hymn book on the shelf in front of her. Even the church cleaning team (that she used to be on) don't have the faintest idea how to clean the seats. And as for what they call a cup of tea these days . . . !

Suggested Response. Is Annie a Christian? Has anyone ever truly tried to help Annie commit her life to the Lord? Sometimes older people who come to church are never challenged on this. Possibly, because of this, the church's teaching means little to Annie. Perhaps one or two people could really work out a pastoral strategy for her, taking a special note of her on Sundays. They could offer her patience and love, reaffirm her in the eyes of her friends, use their testimony of Jesus, sit with her at coffee time and listen, whether they agree or not with what she says.

Marian

The Situation. Marian is about to leave the church. She feels really hurt. Her husband died unexpectedly leaving her a widow at 63. The funeral was beautiful and people were kind. Her husband did a lot for the church one way and another and Marian supported him loyally. However, she seems now to be in a new category. Groups form over coffee and somehow she is on the edge of them. Events take place – a barbecue, for example, in a friend's garden – and she no longer seems to hear about them. She isn't quite sure where to sit in church. She doesn't like being alone in a row and yet can't decide quickly where to go. She and Derek led their own housegroup of a few elderly people, but it lapsed in the weeks leading up to the funeral, and somehow she does not feel she can go on with it.

Suggested Response. Are there any (trained) "bereavement visitors" in the church? Not her particular friends but others who can listen and just "be there"? Can one or two people unobtrusively take on the question of where Marian sits at church? Can people treat her normally and not avoid her, not knowing what to say? Perhaps this is the time to realize that, in your church, couples tend to think in couples and single people are often simply left out of some events. Can the coordinator of the house-groups take it upon himself/herself to look into the matter of Marian's former housegroup? Perhaps another leader could be found to help lead it, or it might be better for Marian to link into another one.

Peggy

The Situation. There isn't a problem really, except that she is overworked and unacknowledged. She runs the Tuesday Afternoon Fellowship and does a really good job although she has a very tough time finding good speakers. She tries to keep tabs on the older people that aren't so well. She washes up after the fellowship meet-ings. She cleans the place up since "mums and tots" are due there at nine o'clock on Thursday, and she quietly visits in the residential home near the church. Peggy doesn't complain when the leaders of the youth work, and those who "give the chalice" at Holy Communion, and the "ministry team"; and "those going to Spring Harvest", and so on, are all called up to the front of the church from time to time and prayed over. It doesn't occur to her that she should be there. It doesn't occur to anyone else either.

At the end of the annual church meeting she can give

a brief report on the Tuesday Afternoon Fellowship. "Keep it short, won't you, Peggy, dear? They'll be worn out by then." After all, it's only a fellowship for a few old people.

I suppose this is why this chapter has had to be written at all.

I conclude with a list made from many genuine "audience-response" sheets. The information was collected from many seminars and workshops on reaching older people for Christ.

The question asked was: "What are older people expected to do in the church, and what would they like to do?" The following answers repeated themselves many times.

Older people in church are expected to: Pray, be tolerant, accept changes, stand down from the church council, keep up with the young, make tea, not rock the boat, do flowers, not talk about the past, help with the crèche, "sit up, shut up, and pay up", knit squares, dust, hand out books, run the Mothers' Union, organize the bazaar or jumble sale, mend the church furnishings, polish the brass, do church maintenance and office work, (simple, not computers. Sticking on stamps variety).

Older people would like to: Help others, share experiences, use talents, listen to older hymns, be loved, be recognized as part of the church family, be listened to, pray, be involved in decision-making, share more activities in the general church, be part of the visiting programme, help the handicapped, be a granny figure in the crèche, take part in hospital or prison visiting, be in a home group, take services in old people's homes, counsel, teach, evangelize, help children in school, help with publicity, keep identity, have a clear ministry, share wisdom, have links with younger people, not clean brass, have a voice in things, lead worship sometimes, be part of a pastoral care team, be part of all events, be a prayer partner with a young person, learn how to pray for each other.

There's quite a lot there to think about. Why is it that older people are so seldom recognized as people who can do such things? Is the church family really at fault or have we sometimes just begun to "opt out" in our spiritual growth and so have less to offer?

It's good to ask ourselves, sometimes: how is "being an older person" affecting our Christian life? Here is a way to check on yourselves: a "spiritual health check" if you like. Be honest. No one need see it but you although you might like to work through it with one or two friends, and don't be discouraged at a "low score". We all "opt out" sometimes. Look up the suggested Bible verses give at the end, and hang in there!

Is old age a time to opt out? A spiritual health check

For each number select the statement which *most nearly* reflects your thinking: (Be honest. No one sees it but you.)

(1) (a) I expect to serve the Lord with what gifts I have until he takes me to himself in heaven.

    (b) I've done my bit as a Christian worker. Let others take up the challenge. I'll serve on the sidelines.

    (c) I can't do much for the Lord these days. It's all I can do to get to church.

(2) (a) I believe that I can still be a witness to the saving grace of the Lord Jesus and lead others to him.

    (b) I used to work in evangelism when I was younger, but this is the task of others now.

    (c) I am not so sure now that I could lead someone else to Jesus. Even the church leaders don't seem very sure what it means.

(3) (a) I know the Lord has a perfect plan for my life and that I am still walking in it.

    (b) The Lord has led me faithfully to this time and now my job is to wait for my homecall as patiently as I can.

    (c) I am beginning to be very frightened by the possibility of illness and dependence on others.

(4) (a) I believe that my fears and frustrations at growing older can be taken away by the Lord and that I can still find joy in life.

    (b) I think, as Christians, we should be able to put up with the problems of old age.

    (c) I do have some really low moments. Sometimes God seems so far away!

(5) (a) I believe I can grow in my knowledge and love of his word, and go on growing!

    (b) Of course I read my Bible portion every day and I always enjoy the Sunday sermons.

(c) I don't do much real Bible study now. But I repeat verses to myself sometimes.

(6) (a) I believe that prayer is vital to my health and growth as a Christian. So I pray.

(b) I have a little prayer each morning, asking God to help me through the day.

(c) I don't pray much these days.

(7) (a) I believe that my physical and spiritual needs will be met as I take them to the Lord in prayer.

(b) I try not to worry about money and other things but I do wake at night sometimes and my problems seem very large.

(c) Life isn't easy and I worry a lot about how expensive things are getting.

(8) (a) I believe in a bright future that is not too far away!

(b) I do expect to go to heaven but I try not to think much about death. It's rather a gloomy topic, isn't it?

(c) I suppose I'll go to heaven. I've always been a Christian and tried to help others.

(9) (a) I believe that prayer can change things across the world so I often pray for others.

(b) I pray for my family, of course, but not often for anyone else.

(c) I hardly ever spend time praying for others.

(10) (a) I do ask God to help me know what I can do about the needy people we hear about.

(b) I'm sorry for others with problems, but there is little I can do at my age.

(c) I'm really fed up with all these appeals coming through the door. There's nothing I can do about them.

Now let's add up your score!

Score 2 for every (a); 1 for every (b); and 0 for every (c). If you have scored 18–20: hold fast to what you have! If you have scored 12–17, you could be beginning to "opt out" a little. Please look up the Bible verses below which relate to the numbers for which you could not select (a). Think them over!

If you have scored less than 12 (specially in 5c) give some time to study prayerfully the verses that follow and perhaps ask your church if they could find you a large-print Bible. Opting out or not, we are still part of God's family on earth. There's a lot ahead.

Verses relating to numbers above:

1. 1 Corinthians 15:58; John 4:14; Philippians 1:6; Psalm 92.12–15
2. 2 Corinthians 2.14–16; 2 Corinthians 4.1.5–6; 1 Peter 2:5
3. Romans 8:14; Psalm 32:8; 48:14.
4. 2 Corinthians 12:9–10; 1 Corinthians 10:13; Romans 14:17.
5. 2 Timothy 2:15; 2 Corinthians 4:14,16,18; Romans 4:20–21, and 7.22.
6. 1 Thessalonians 5:16–18; Matthew 7:7–8; Colossians 4:2

7. Isaiah 40:29–31; 46:3–4; Psalm 18:2–4,6; Philippians 4:6,19; 2 Corinthians 9:8.
8. Hebrews 6:19–20; 1 Peter 5:10; James 1:12; 1 John 5.11–13; 1 Corinthians 2.9.
9. 1 Thessalonians 5:11; Philippians 1:3–5; Ephesians 6:18; Galatians 6:2.
10. 1 John 3:17; Romans 12:11; 2 Corinthians 1:3–4; 1 John 4:7.

CHAPTER FIVE

SERVICES IN RESIDENTIAL AND NURSING HOMES

Let's go straight in.

Please note that the following scenes are entirely (well, almost entirely) fictional.

We arrive at Rest Haven, all four of us, about fifteen minutes before the time when the service is meant to start. We ring the bell (since we haven't had the code number given to us) and go in. The entrance hall is warm and pleasant with some flowers around. On the left, the manager nods a greeting from her office. A mound of paperwork is on her desk. Down the hall, one of the carers comes hurrying towards us, sees us, and turns back promptly, muttering, "Must get Annie to the toilet." A cleaner, pushing the carpet sweeper in the main lounge where we have the service, just scowls.

We take off our coats and go into the lounge. There are two residents there, both asleep. However, some friendly staff are bringing in some others in wheel chairs, and Bob – who never quite knows where he is these days – wanders in with a smile and turns the television on. The cleaner and her carpet sweeper move a little nearer the door.

Though it may not look like it, they are prepared for us and we are on time. We have been coming here for about a year now. The minister of our church got permission for us to come and take a Christian service here on the first and third Sunday of the month at 11.30 a.m. It is the only contact with a church they seem to have. We keep to time.

The matron appears and greets us. Our leader, John, asks her how Maureen (one of the residents) is today.

"She's not too good," the matron replies. "I doubt if she'll manage the service, but go up and see her if you like. We can get her down if you think she'd like to come."

John and Helen go up to the first floor to see Maureen, and Ann and I say hello to Bob and the two ladies in wheel chairs and begin to put the other chairs into some kind of a circle. We move the keyboard out from the wall. Ann is the reluctant pianist. She's not great, but (as she says) better than nothing.

There are different views about the hymn singing. At first we had brought some old *Ancient and Modern* hymn-books from a cupboard in the church that everyone had forgotten about. Every time a hymn was announced, we went around finding the numbers for everyone who was fumbling – until we realized that it wasn't the numbers that most of them couldn't see, but the words. After that we found some large print hymnbooks, quite light to handle. They work better, although I know a friend who just uses good cassette tapes: a single voice singing well-known hymns with each word clear. Generally I think more people join in those than manage to read the words in any hymnbook. Some people give out sheets of the hymns that they are going to use each time, in big print. The plus is that people can keep them and perhaps look at them later in the day. The minus is that it is yet another sheet of paper.

It is sometimes very moving to see that even those with different forms of dementia will sing the hymns, a memory perhaps of earlier days. I remember Joe, who never said anything and appeared to know no one, but when we sang the hymn "Nearer My God to Thee" he came alive and joined in perfectly. It's still "that genera-tion", isn't it? In another 20 years or so, they won't be there. On the other hand, that's me, isn't it? So maybe we will. Others can be more disruptive. Vera is capable of shouting out, "Shut your racket!" in the middle of a hymn, which takes some getting used to.

John and Helen are praying with Maureen in her little room on the first floor. Maureen is a member of our church. It had been a real shock when she had a stroke some months back and had to be taken into care. She always sat in the second row on the left at the nine o'clock Sung Eucharist, and I suppose we thought she always would. When she was moved to Rest Haven, for a while we had arranged for someone to pick her up and bring her to church, but somehow it just tailed off. It was then she asked the matron if we could come and take a regular service. That's how we happen to be here at all.

I've discovered since that Christians gain entrance into residential homes simply because a Christian resident asks if there could be a service on a Sunday. But there aren't many churches willing to do it regularly. Carols at

Christmas, that's what people like doing. Cheering up the old folks and bringing indigestible mince pies just when they have their relatives with them and the home has put on a really nice spread. But to take a service once a week or once a fortnight? That's different. That's a commitment and, after all, Sundays are precious, aren't they? "We're expecting our . . . er . . . well . . . we are a bit busy."

Our congregation is now growing a little as the carers help them in and get them seated. Most of them are the regulars and we greet each other. I'm leading the service today so I smile at Bob, who is still wandering around, and give him a hymnbook, hoping he won't notice I'm turning off the television. John and Helen come back without Maureen. But I know she'll be praying for us.

I say where we come from and who we are, even if we've done it every time. After all, why should they remember? They only see us once a fortnight. But I rather like saying, "I'm Rhena and this is John, and Helen and Ann." After all, most of them seem to lose their surnames when they get into places like this and have become Hilda, and Emily and Kathleen . . . So we lose ours, too. And I say it loudly. (God has blessed me with a loud voice, or is it the teacher in me showing again?)

So many people make the mistake of thinking they are heard by older people when they are not. They get to a microphone, perhaps in a church hall, and find it isn't working. "Oh dear," they say, tapping it professionally. "It doesn't seem to be working. Never mind. You can all hear me, can't you?" Because there is no response, they carry on cheerfully.

Older people in church have got used to "not hearing". I once bravely said to a young minister, "Do you realize, Derek, that you speak very softly when you are in the pulpit? There are a lot of people who are not hearing you."

He looked at me, unimpressed. "The old ones, you mean? Well, I'm not going to shout just for them," he said.

Then I announce a hymn, "Oh Worship the Lord", and Ann gets rather shakily going on the keyboard. One Sunday she pressed the "drum-accompaniment" key by mistake and then couldn't see which one it was to turn it off. It really went down well with "Abide with me".

It's not easy always to get the right sort of service together for these events. It so much depends who is in front of you, and it can be a bewildering group of people.

- Wilfred was a wing commander in the first world war. He can't get out of his chair unaided, but he is definitely "all there" and likely to be extremely critical of any sloppiness in the service.
- Marjory tells us she lived in the same "down town" area for over 80 years and had (so she explains) three husbands (presumably one after the other) and a large family. I've only seen a rather sad-looking elderly niece come to see her. She is always grumbling that she can't smoke.
- Bert worked on the railway and tells us every time that he's "chapel". Angela (one of the Featherstone-Haughs) stares silently into space and says nothing, even when we sit by her and try to talk. I long to know

what distant view she sees. Some sing a little or follow
the lines in the book. Others sit silent.

We have to make up our minds when we do this sort of
thing. Are we bringing a sort of replica of a church
service? Are we coming, as it were, to bring a sense of
"difference" and "sanctity" into the home? Some teams
bring a candle into the room as a visible sign that something different is going on. Robes might be worn by the
leader if this is appropriate to your tradition. Holy communion could be offered. Or should it be less formal, a
friendly visit by Christians, perhaps with lively music,
impromptu prayers and maybe some dramatic readings
or small plays? Only you can know the right approach to
a particular home.

On this visit, because we come from an Anglican
church, I have copied a prayer from the Prayer Book and,
after the hymn, John reads it for me. "Holy Father, give us
a spirit of contentment and peace, whatever our circumstances: that we may accept who we are and what we
have. Bless those who help us and befriend us. Bless the
members of our families, specially those far away from
us. And give us peace in our hearts and a freedom from
worry and despair. Through Jesus Christ our Lord.
Amen." Then we say the Lord's Prayer together and there
is a short Bible reading.

Each home is different in atmosphere, in kindness or
hopelessness, peace or anxiety. This is not a matter of the
staff who, in my experience, are usually kind and doing
the best they can. More, it is a matter of the older people

there and what is going on in their inner thoughts: their grief, resentment, feeling of loss, uncertainty, loneliness, or fear. When you are holding a service, feel the atmosphere and ask Jesus to be there with you. He does not pass it by. God has a special heart for the weak and helpless, young and old.

I have also gone with others into a big room of the mentally infirm. There has been a sort of quiet restlessness in the room. There is anxiety there, some muttering complaints, others crying, even shouting occasionally. But, as we begin and the name of Jesus is mentioned and God is brought into the picture, some quietness falls. Not entirely. Some can still call out, but I have thought sometimes that we have brought an awareness of the presence of Jesus into that room. He is walking around it, caring, loving, calming.

Bible reading helps too. The Word of God is not just me (or someone else) reading from the Bible. This is the Word of God, and the Holy Spirit is our Counsellor and Teacher as we read it. Read clearly a passage from the Bible, and pray as you leave, "When we've gone, Holy Spirit, bring these words back to them."

Today I have chosen a reading from John 14. I like to use more than one voice if I can and have asked John to read "Jesus" and Helen to be "Thomas". I explain that this passage is when Jesus is about to be arrested and crucified. He knows he is going to leave the disciples and is trying to comfort his friends so that they don't lose faith in him when he leaves them.

So they read:

JESUS   Don't let your hearts be troubled. Trust in
             God and trust also in me. In my Father's
             house are many rooms; if it were not so, I
             would have told you. I am going there to
             prepare a place for you. And if I go and
             prepare a place for you I will come back and
             take you to be with me that you also may be
             where I am. You know the way to the place
             where I am going.

NARRATOR (Me) Thomas, a disciple said to him:

THOMAS   Lord, we don't know where you are going, so
             how can we know the way?

NARRATOR   And Jesus answered:

JESUS   I am the way and the truth and the life. No
             one comes to the Father except through me.

Having more than one voice brings variety to the reading.

In the "sermon" or "talk" I take the first line of the
words of Jesus above. I speak briefly about the need to
trust in Jesus when things get rough or when we are
worried about members of our family or what's going to
happen in the future. Sometimes we really don't understand why God has let this or that happen, but he still asks
us for our trust.

"It's not so difficult to do," I say. "We trust in things we
don't understand all the time." I had a flashlight in my
hand. "I trust it," I said. "When I want to read the bus
timetable in the evening or find my car door when I have
parked it in the dark, I take this out. I don't understand
how it works, how to make a battery or why that bulb

lights up. But I trust the person who made it. We don't understand why things happen as they do on earth, but we have to learn to *trust* God, knowing that the way to reach him is through Jesus, who said I am the way, the truth and the life . . ."

Now that is not the best sermon in the world. You could do a lot better, I'm sure, but it was done this way because, in homes that are not specifically Christian, it is the type of sermon that will be heard. It is short and makes one point that, when we have left, someone might remember.

Take care that you don't sound as if you are talking to children. You are stating a serious fact, sowing a seed, giving a thought. Anything further can take place when you talk to individuals afterwards. Pray as you leave that the Holy Spirit will bring back the words to comfort and encourage them.

We sing another hymn. Sometimes after that we pray a prayer of confession. Can we help those who have such bitter memories, such fear, such a sense of helplessness? I pray simply and use the familiar and comforting words afterwards: "Almighty God, who forgives all who truly repent, have mercy upon us. Pardon and deliver us from all our sins, confirm and strengthen us in all godliness, and keep us in life eternal through Jesus Christ our Lord. Amen." Then I pray for others, often mentioning any special need in the home. Another hymn follows, and a final prayer.

Ann plays on softly for a while, just to keep the atmosphere still. The rest of us go quietly from one to another, shaking hands or just laying a hand on them and saying a prayer. Some share needs and special fears. A relative might be there, worried because she has heard her husband is going to be moved next week. Perhaps there is someone new. Do not hurry. For a short while the room has been still, without the persistent clamour of the television. Hearts are quieted and comforted. This is a work worth doing.

But where is "evangelism" in all this? Sometimes just left out.

Can we learn from Paul?

Let me tell you a little about Paul. About 20 years ago, an old lady came up to Paul, then a deacon in a local church, and asked him if he would visit her in the residential home where she lived. "It kind of snowballed after that," Paul explained. "I started visiting others who asked me to come. Then they would move to another home and that opened another door."

Gradually this work took over Paul's life, and for over 10 years now he has been doing it full-time, covering over 20 homes a week.

Paul is a loner. Others join him for a day sometimes and get some vision themselves of the need he sees so plainly; but he is the one who comes every week without fail. "This is my Sunday," an old lady said to me once when I went with him. It was a Tuesday afternoon. I asked him recently how he managed to give so many talks without getting stale. "I have a theme each month," he answered. "One month I used the 'unique' things about Jesus: a unique birth, a unique death (when others had a reason for the punishment and he was perfect and without sin), and a unique resurrection. Another time, I took his miracles, and so on."

His talks are short and simple, using everyday situations. There are highly educated people in Paul's audience, but somehow he doesn't offend. Maybe they are too tired now for complicated sermons, and Paul is kind. His kindness shows through as he gets up to help someone shuffle out of the room, or picks up a book, or holds someone's hand to pray with them. "Paul's coming is the highlight of the week," one said to me.

Paul is straightforward when it comes to urging people to make a commitment to Jesus. You see that door over there, he might say. You can't get out of here unless you go through it, can you? Well, I want to tell you there's a door into heaven and Jesus is that door. He said it himself, when he was on earth. I am the door, he said, and he that enters in by me will be saved. You can make that choice today if you want to. Can I ask you to just raise your hand if you want to give your life to Jesus?

When I was with him in one of the homes a wavering hand went up. "Perhaps she does it every time," I thought. But Paul prayed over her and blessed her. Afterwards he wrote her name in his little book. "I've waited a long time for Alice to make that decision," he said to me. He will now treat her as a Christian, sure of salvation.

I asked him about others who had given their lives to Christ. He told me about two others. His own words follow:

- There was a gentleman of 98 in a home I went to who was at first very hostile when I came into the room. When the matron gave me permission to turn off the television he would curse and swear at me and stump off to his room. One day he wasn't there. I went to visit him in his room and he just said to me, "Paul, I'd like to be like Jesus", and I had the privilege of leading him to Christ.

- Another time one of the Christian staff in a home took me in to see a lady of 104 who had newly arrived. She asked who I was and Gill told her I was a Christian preacher. "I don't want anyone to preach at me!" she said. I said "I haven't come to preach, but I want to tell you about someone who cares for you and loves you and who died for you." She said, "Who's that, then?" and I told her about Jesus, and she gave her life to him there and then. Soon after she died.

Paul estimates that in his years of service he has seen over 500 older people give their lives to Jesus.

We are not all Pauls, and this "man in a million" has had his share of criticism and discouragement; but I still think his namesake in the New Testament would have taken him to his heart. And I wish with all my heart that we, who go Sunday after Sunday into residential and nursing homes, were more open to the prompting of the Spirit and had more courage to say more often, "Have you given your life into the hands of Jesus and accepted his death for you on the cross and, if not, would you do it now?"

It is often at the end of our service that these vital few words can be exchanged. Here, to close this chapter, is a testimony of one couple:

At the end of one meeting, Vera (who had been continually disruptive throughout the meeting, often shouting out, "Shut your racket!" during the hymns) grabbed hold of my wife's hand and said she wanted to be saved. My wife prayed with her and she received the Lord's salvation. Then her neighbour asked to be prayed for. She said she felt so changed and had received so much from the meetings. Vera was changed too. She still shouted out, but now it was, "Be quiet! I can't hear the meeting!" I often think of her and the verse in Revelation 3.15, where God says to the Laodicean church, "You are neither cold nor hot. I wish you were either one or the other!"

Sadly both these ladies have died since but are, thank God, with Him.

This is a ministry where often the gate into eternal life is particularly close. Let us take it seriously.

Contributors to this chapter: Paul Gunstone (Bexhill-on-Sea, UK); Tony and Faith Hayles (New Life Christian Church, Emsworth, Hampshire, UK); The team from All Saints Church, Harpenden, Herts, UK; and many others who have shared with me over the years.

CHAPTER SIX

WAKING UP THE WEDNESDAY AFTERNOON FELLOWSHIP

Let's start by confessing that sometimes these meetings do need a shot in the arm. Probably any leader reading this would agree. "Oh, for some new ideas, a famous and wonderful speaker who doesn't charge anything, a little more appreciation shown by those who come, and three or four more helpers!" What's the real purpose of the meeting, anyway?

In fact, the "Wednesday afternoon fellowship" (hereafter referred to as W.A.F.), or its equivalent in the church programme, could have quite an important reason for existence. Speaking generally, meetings like this usually exist primarily to bring people together in a comfortable and friendly place where they meet people they know, have a laugh, and enjoy a good cup of tea. It could be the only social contact some of the members have during the week, and it is important to them.

Often, understandably, it is the older retired people who come to them. The 50+ generation are either at work, coping with teenagers, or busy staffing charity shops, running the church coffee bar and/or office, or collecting

for Christian Aid. It has sometimes been said that chari-
ties would simply fold up and die were it not for the 50+s
and their commitment to them.

If the W.A.F. is held in a church by Christians, a second
and equally acceptable purpose will be "friendship evangelism" perhaps in the hope that some members who
never think of going to church these days might like to re-
consider, or come to a special weekday service if available. Older people are so often "expecting the family" on
a Sunday.

All this is fine. Don't let me discourage you, but the title
of this chapter is *"Waking up" the Wednesday Afternoon
Fellowship*, so let's centre on that. If you feel your meeting
is awake enough already, then skip this chapter and try
the next.

Considering and meeting needs

On the whole, "movement and change" take place where
there has been a real effort to consider people's needs and
how to meet them. Wednesday Afternoon Fellowships
would not exist at all if people didn't need each other to
talk to, to laugh and cry with, to learn from and be encouraged by, to share problems with, and so on. And somewhere along the line I expect that the needs of the leaders
and helpers are also being met by leading such a group.

Take a step further. What about other more universal
needs people might have in this world of ours? Could we
do a little "waking up" within our fellowship if we set out
to meet them?

A well-known and oft-quoted listing of needs comes from Abraham Maslow's "hierarchy of needs". As one is met, we move to the next:

1. Physical needs, i.e., food, shelter etc.
2. Safety and security
3. Social acceptance, i.e., to feel a sense of belonging
4. Esteem/respect of others
5. Self-fulfilment

Using this as a guide, we can think about these needs as they relate to the members of our own meeting and ask whether our planned programme of speakers and activities is addressing them.

Physical needs and the need for security

Let us take (1) and (2) together as the basic needs of having enough to eat and a house which is not falling down around us; and feeling reasonably secure within the house and generally safe when venturing out.

You may, of course, be in an area where these matters are not an anxiety to the older people in your meeting, but think it through before you dismiss them. Remember it is not necessarily a question of money. Sometimes it is one of pride.

For example, we are not quick to admit (a) That our sitting room only has a side light because the central light bulb has gone and we are not steady enough to get on a chair to replace it. (b) That the garden fence has been kicked in by children again and the man who used to mend it died last winter. (c) That the kitchen tap has been constantly dripping for the last three months and the local plumber (if he exists) couldn't be less interested. (d) That we can't get to the supermarket at all these days because the neighbour who used to take us is ill. (e) That we are worried sick because a knee operation has been delayed for the tenth time and now we just can't manage the stairs.

Need I go on? These matters are desperately important and sometimes very easily dealt with. But have we built up enough of a friendship with our members to get to know about them? And do we have a "Fred" or "Bert" or "Marian" who doesn't mind helping out? Of course the last one listed above is not so easily dealt with, but loving sympathy goes a long way.

Incidentally it has always amazed me how cruel older people can be about one another. "That Mrs Wilson! Moan! moan! moan! If she'd had my bad leg for the last four years, she'd have something to moan about! What makes her so special?" I am left speechless watching this kind of thing, and to fight it, reprove it, and eliminate it needs to be a matter of prayer and action for a fellowship leader. A group can be poisoned by that attitude.

But let us look at the other levels of need:

Social acceptance or the need to belong

We do not need to look very closely into our present society to realize that growing old can lead to a retreat into a kind of ghetto: the ghetto of old age. Unless we are of interest to the advertisers because we are in the class of WOOPIES (well-off older people) or JOLLIES (jet-setting oldsters with lots of loot)[1] sometimes we can feel we are not of great interest to anyone. If the family is nearby, it is good of course, but many families are split and scattered today.

This is where the W.A.F. clearly has something to offer. It is something to belong to. Your name is known, even if sometimes you rapidly have to become "Mildred" or "Frank" to total strangers. And it means you can look out for each other. News about one another can be shared for prayer and possible action. Nancy, for example, is not well. She has succumbed to the flu going around. Bob and Shirley actually met the Prime Minister last week. Marjory had a fall in the public library and didn't feel she should come out today. Gloria has a seventeenth grand-child. It's George's birthday today and so on.

My experience of such fellowships is that this is an important part of their service to the community. But be practical, not paternalistic. You don't want to put the above in the same category as IT'S JOHN'S TURN TO DO THE WEATHER CHART TODAY on the schoolroom wall.

The important thing is that someone cares. We all need someone to tell things to. I can remember an older lady who had had her handbag snatched one afternoon on her own street. She was shaken and crying when she got home, but there was no one to tell.

So if you are one of the leaders of the group, remember: membership matters. Work on getting to know people, spend time with them and help them get to know each other.

There are lots of ways of doing this: an attractive membership or programme card, a list of special prayer requests handed around every week, a "Come and join us" card to give to members to invite their friends, and so on. There is a great deal that the W.A.F. can do to meet the need of "belonging".

That's even more important these days because of the struggle older people often have to belong to today's world at all. This is, in fact, another "belonging need" our fellowship can try to address: The need to feel part of today's world.

I was at a large Christian event (I have genuinely forgotten which). The speaker was speaking with passion from the platform, and his theme was the reluctance and apathy in the Christian church to reach the "people of our time" with the gospel. I do not, of course, remember the exact words, but the message came across.

"We must look with urgency at our churches that appear to have no relevance for the people of our time!" he challenged us. Do we try to understand their thinking, their priorities, their needs in a culture totally unlike the one we are used to? Do we recognize our responsibility for the people of our time, or will we remain as the unchanging church relevant only to a world which no longer exists? And so on. You get the idea. He must have mentioned the "people of our time" in just about every sentence. OK, I did know what group of people he was referring to, and I'm sure he was right. But I just wished he had chosen another phrase because, if I was sure of any thing, I was certain he didn't mean me.

And yet, are we not "people of our time"? There are today over 10.6 million people of pensionable age in the UK, which represents 18.2% of the total population. Other Western countries have similar proportions. So get used to the idea. We (for I am in this age group) are here, in big numbers. "I'm afraid our congregation is mainly older people," a minister said when I arrived to speak on "missionary work in Kenya", and missed the soft growl I was giving even then. Who likes to be apologized for? Admittedly, we are seen sometimes today as a hindrance to church growth, rather than a help to it. But whose fault is that, and who is interested in helping us understand and react to the changes around us? Possibly the church could take us on board too, in its struggle to "get a grip on the future"? We are, after all, probably going to live through a lot more of it than we could have expected to in the last century.

The need to belong to life today, to still contribute something somewhere, is a real one to pensioners – if it's not too late. I talked this over with an older friend. She wrote me a note the next day: "How necessary is it to try and belong to 'today's world'? Many older people have not been part of 'today's world' for a long time and do not want to be part of it today. And how much is possible anyway?"

Which makes me all the more determined to raise the subject. What can the W.A.F. do to help its members to look beyond themselves and their personal needs, into the world in which they (still) live?

Let's check your programme in this context.

Speakers: I accept that the search for good speakers is an on-going problem. But among your usual list, try to cross generations more often. Don't always feel you have to reach back into the past.

Shirley Toulson in her excellent book *The Country of Old Age*[2] mentions the "all too often mistaken and well-meaning 'carers' – friends, neighbours and relations" – who "seem to push the old back into the past, not out of any genuine desire for knowledge but out of some mis-guided notion that it would be good for the old to relive their youth in this way." (p. 59)

Memories are precious, and looking backwards at the war years, or the songs you sang and the things you laughed at in the 30s or 40s does have its place. But to go back too often into the past may confirm your members in the view that they are "of the past". Try some topics that speak of today.

Find some speakers from today's workplace. It isn't always easy since the meeting is in the afternoon, but it may not be impossible. Mix with your usual list of speakers people like:

1. A parent of teenagers to speak honestly on the problems and joys parents have to deal with today and how they differ from their own childhood memories. (We don't have to get ALL our input from soaps and daytime chat shows).
2. A number of (friendly!) young people to instruct on the "language" of today (no holds barred).

3. Someone working in, for example, a supermarket. What goes on behind the scenes? What is the "career ladder" you climb? What are the worst things that can happen?
4. A disabled person with a witness and a readiness to discuss attitudes and language that offends.
5. A school teacher on how schools are changing.
6. "My worst day" or (if recently appointed) "my first day" in some job.
7. An asylum seeker with a story to tell of settling into England.
   . . . and so on.

Discussion groups: According to Toulson (p. 41): "If a person cannot even afford to keep warm, clean, properly housed and fed, then it is ridiculous to try to turn to philosophical questions."

However, if they *are* "warmed and fed" there could be room occasionally for a discussion group, perhaps prior to the meeting. In one church, this was called the "Seekers" group. This might be another way of introducing W.A.F. members to the questions being asked today. One idea would be to pick up some of the issues raised in the soaps. Sometimes these discussion groups become regular pre-meeting gatherings which could turn into Bible studies as people seek to see what the Bible has to say about the problems facing them today.

Are you getting the idea? The above suggestions are ways of saying: "This is the world we live in, and we all are in it, the young and the old. We are all trying to make the best we can of the cards we have been dealt at this point of our history. Don't drop out!"

So now we come to the next need.

The need for self-respect, and the esteem of others

It is sometimes hard for an older person today to feel they could ever be admired or esteemed by the modern world. And yet most of us have known older people who stayed in our minds as people who enriched our lives, whom we have loved and respected right to the end. Why? Because they have remained "persons" in their own right with much to give.

Our society today gives "things" (money, good housing, power dressing, travel, prestige, possessions) priority over persons, and has built up a civilization around it. Old people are discounted because they are purely and simply persons and are no longer of much importance to the architects of this world.

However, maybe it is older people today who can show us that there are situations where to be "just people" is great. For example, for some the world of grandparents is a special one. In the town where I live there is a central large common. Every morning, if the sun is shining, the common is taken over by the grandparents and the children they are caring for, while the parents work. Most look entirely happy. It can give us unexpected flashes of joy to find within ourselves the skill to fill a human need or to create something of beauty: to feel the wood in our hands, to watch the clay turning on the wheel, to see a scene of beauty springing to life under our hands as we draw or paint. Suddenly we have time to be people. There is no rat race.

Yes, we can find satisfaction within ourselves, but there is another need: to be admired and respected for what we offer to life as a whole, not only to immediate family or neighbours, or even to ourselves, but to the community as a whole. The W.A.F. should make room for action and involvement in the world as well as offer opinions.

"Teams within a team": If you have a fairly large group, you might consider the formation of "special interest" groups within it. Here are some very brief suggestions as to the kind of group I mean.

- Could a small number visit a nearby residential or nursing home fairly regularly, just to offer friendship? Maybe someone plays an instrument or sings well, or makes beautiful things they could take and share with the residents. I can remember a couple who contributed an entirely patient and well-behaved dog to the visit. It was always popular.
- Some could be the fellowship's "prayer team", listing and praying for things mentioned by members of the fellowship, visiting those ill, or getting up to date news about them, and producing cards with special requests for prayer on them.
- How about a drama team? (The W.A.F. players in action!) There is scope for short skits or plays that could be performed at the W.A.F. meeting or to the church at large or to day-centres around the town (see chapter 11).

- An Information Technology group. Getting to know a computer. An introduction to the Internet. There are people around ready to introduce older people to these things if you look for them hard enough! In America the highest usage of the e-mail network is among those over 65.

- The "organizers". Is there a holiday coming? An outing? A special presentation somewhere, maybe from the drama group or the art and craft group? Who plans the programme for the W.A.F., anyway?

- The art and craft group. This may just be a group of those who have gifts in the area of embroidery, knitting, toy-making, model-making, pottery, glass-painting and so on. It would be an opportunity to display progress, to advise or help one another. Possibly there could be things they could do for the church: such as covering or embroidering "kneelers" which are less common today but some churches use. Maybe banners or flags are popular or perhaps they could meet just to enjoy one another's gifts and creativity.

- The media group, who study the local papers together to write letters of affirmation or protest. What causes can be taken up? Are the W.A.F. presented frequently and positively in the church magazine or newspaper? Is there a church notice board that they could contribute to? Do they need to write to the BBC about something? Join a protest locally? Take up and collect for a special charity? See what use can be made of the local radio stations.

- The writers' group. Those who enjoy writing prose or poetry or have started on a book can meet to share ideas, formats, illustrations, or possible publishers. Certainly they can read to one another and share opinions.

Any of the above can attract interest and praise if done well, and also help members know and respect each other's gifts. It is this that fulfils the fourth "need" as listed above (for self-respect and the esteem of others). Remember: there is nothing like working together to create real friendships.

As I write this a strong picture comes to mind of a W.A.F. leader, having read through the above, saying in despair, "But I can't get anyone even to read a Bible passage to the meeting, let alone do all that!" Just be open to the idea. Start with one or two interest groups. God opens doors in his time and in his way.

The final need: self-fulfilment. Under this we must include: the need of yielding to Christ (in whom all needs are met)

Let me ask you two questions:

1. Are you encouraging evangelism as part of the mission statement of the W.A.F.? Or, put in another way, do you want your members to put their faith in Christ as Saviour and Lord of their lives?
2. Are you helping the Christians in the W.A.F. to grow in their faith?

Chapters 2–4 of this book have a lot to say about this. Perhaps you could have another look at them specially with your meeting in mind.

I wonder how you are feeling as you reach the end of this chapter? If you are still discouraged – and this sounds a really bad note to end on – maybe you should have the courage to close down. We need to recognize the word S-T-O-P sometimes when meetings have gone on for years, a constant burden on unwilling people, and are achieving nothing.

But – on the other hand – if all the Wednesday Afternoon Fellowships suddenly ceased to be, there would be a lot of lonely people around. So take it to the Lord in prayer and see if anything suggested here might help. Recognize that this part of service to the church is as important as any other. Feel good about it. God cares for the weak and the lonely . . . so do you.

Ideas for your meeting

Invite speakers on the following subjects

- A local history lesson
- Questions of health. How to keep fit. Exercises to do at home, diet, caring for your feet, hair, eyes, ears etc. Advice, demonstration, participation
- Local PC – bogus callers
- Paragliding (perhaps with a video?). Or another not-too-common sport explained and perhaps illustrated
- Bereavement

- Bird-watching (and feeding)
- Torch fellowship and their books
- Writing a poem. How to start
- Modern "hymns" and how to enjoy them (a music group can come in to teach them)
- Today's fashion (perhaps with the help of a local shop)
- How to take photos
- Things that make me laugh
- Learning a new craft/hobby (Flower arranging? Woodwork? A study of antiques?)
- Banner-making
- Armchair gardening
- My holiday and its best – or worst – moments
- Words we don't know (Taken by a parent of the young!)
- What is the Internet?
- The stories behind well-known hymns
- How to pray for others. (Perhaps a link could be made with a young person in the church. Maybe someone just starting at University. Or perhaps someone who has had an accident or is about to have an operation, and so on)
- Favourite hymns, pictures, poems, music, etc. and a word on why they chose it. (Perhaps three or four members from the meeting could present this)
- A testimony of an older person come to faith
- Or someone who has got through a hard time with the Lord or has had some special blessing recently, sometimes better if the speakers are "interviewed" by a friend or leader of the meeting

And if you want to change from an invited speaker, here are some other suggestions

- An "Any Questions" sessions, preferably with the local minister in the panel
- A "Songs of Praise"
- A walk around the village with the local historian
- A "competition" with photos of "me as a baby". Can you guess who's who?
- A display of "holiday postcards" (Can you guess the country?)

CHAPTER SEVEN

A "HOLIDAY AT HOME"

Note: Most of the material that follows comes from a number of Outlook members who have organized a Holiday at Home in their different churches. Their names and churches appear at the end of this chapter but are not linked with a particular contribution. (Outlook, which I direct, is a British charity which encourages evangelism among the over 55s.)

Two difficult months in the lives of older people can be December, because of Christmas, and August, because it is the "holiday month" when families pack their cars to travel to the Continent, the government stops governing, the church activities close down and the television goes into what is called the "silly season" when there are endless repeats of "When Time Goes By" or "Dad's Army".

The implication is that anyone who is anyone is doing something in August. So maybe this is the time to hold a Holiday at Home and bring the holiday atmosphere a little nearer home for some older people around who aren't booked for Tenerife or Bournemouth.

Basically, a Holiday at Home is just what it says: a few days of fun, relaxation, laughter and activity specially set up for older people in their own area. It is something that a church, if pressed, can usually offer since the "mums and tots", Women's Institute, basketball team, weight-watchers, and building maintenance committee have all also closed down in August. Certainly there can be an evangelistic side to this, or I would not be writing this chapter, but it can be mixed in with the whole and be a blessing both to church members and to those who have previously had little contact with the church.

A genuine comment afterwards from a church in Surrey:

A very refreshing and warm feeling of fellowship followed this event. We saw God at work in countless ways. It really was an excellent way to mix people. At least one of the workshops has decided to get together again, perhaps monthly. Thirteen out of the 70 people involved were non-churchgoers, and church members have said that now they know it is such good fun, they'll invite other non-churchgoers in the future. (St John the Baptist, Godalming, UK)

Getting started – the audience

Who is going to come? Do you really have a potential audience? One church started with their lunch club members:

We had been running a lunch club which attracted 70 to 80 people each week for about five years. Over two thirds of those attending were not church members. We organised a Holiday at Home first in 1994 and it has become a fairly regular annual event since, with several having become regular church members because of it. (Christ Church, Bromley, Kent, UK)

Another group considered a wider audience by looking closely at the neighbourhood, commenting:

This is a town with a lot of elderly retired people. Many are newcomers, missing friends and family. Many are widowed and living on their own and lonely. Probably a lot of older people were in touch with a church in their younger days but now, in a new place, they are not sure how to make contact again. Perhaps they are not even sure they want to.

The group started from there.

Another simply (and successfully) used the older members of their congregation and their friends.

So make sure that (a) you have a potential "target audience" and (b) you have the prayer support and interest of your own church before getting too far into your plans.

Who will be your team of helpers?

Are there enough people around to help you run the event? Can you get a group from your church to help? (Try not to have the usual ones who make the tea and

coffee every Sunday. They need a rest in August too.)
Clearly the organizing of such an event is going to be
quite hard work. Those of us involved in evangelism
among the elderly learned quite early that the "prince of
darkness" is very good at reducing and disabling potential workers in this neglected mission field!

Is this something God is asking you to do? If it is, start
now!

One or two things to think about:

A title may give you a theme for the event

Titles do help, and we need to avoid the cringe factor.
Because the title is one of the selling points when it comes
to inviting people, you need something you could say
happily to anyone. I don't think I could possibly invite my
80+ neighbour to something called, for example, "Senior
citizens for God". When you have a title, imagine saying
to an elderly person down the street, "We're having an
event called . . . whatever . . . next month at the church. I
wonder if you'd like to come?". If it feels awkward, look
for another title!

You could use, of course, the basic title "A Holiday at
Home" and probably will, but some people get very creative about having a theme to the function, which obviously may influence the title (I'm not quite sure which
comes first). A theme might encourage you to decorate
the hall in a special way. It makes a big difference to a
rather dark and (perhaps) not so beautiful church hall to

have some bright colours around: banners, pictures, displays. Just think, for example, what you could do with the theme "Heavens Above"!

Here are three examples of using a theme for a Holiday at Home from an extremely creative church:

The Everyday Story of Countryfolk

One church decided to have as their theme, for a three-day event, the story of Ruth from the Bible. The story was serialized at the close of each day by a short drama written by one of the team. The general message was "God has a plan for us all and if things go wrong, he is still with us". They decorated with a "Boaz barn" and had some bales of hay and a large mural of a cornfield.

Home and Away

This signified one day at home and the next day "away". For the first day the church hall was transformed into a seaside holiday with a beach scene on the platform complete with sand, shells, sandcastles, fishing rods and nets. A photographic booth enabled members to be pictured in Victorian bathing dress and there were seaside sideshows such as coconut shying and bowling. The walls were decorated with holiday scenes, and flying overhead were some very realistic seagulls. The "Away" part was a coach trip to Eastbourne, described as a "beautiful sunny day complete with a cream tea".

A Complete U-Day

This was a one-day event in August, intended as a "fun day" but at the same time encouraging each member to think of himself/herself with a body, mind, and spirit. The "body" side of the day included some booths around the hall introducing things like foot care, hair care, skills in make-up, etc., and concluding with a general session during which a "professional" panel answered questions on a range of subjects. In the "mind" section they had a book sale, a display of helpful leaflets from social services, and an experienced computer expert on stage. Then for the "spiritual" side, a visitor from another church sang some gospel songs and shared her testimony. Finally, a retired warden of a home for the elderly spoke about the three BPs: Bus Passes (our opportunities), Blood Pressure (our health) and Bible Promises (our faithful God).

Yes, titles are important and if they indicate a possible theme it's a good idea, but a lot of work is involved, and you obviously need to know your audience and the sort of thing they will enjoy. The danger of treating older people like children is very real and sometimes we have to draw a very fine line. Some suggested titles are listed at the end of this chapter.

Here is the somewhat calmer approach of St Leonards, Chesham Bois, UK: The older members of the congregation were invited to meet daily at the Parish Centre from August 21–25. Encouraged by a poster in the hall to "Have a Whale of a Time", between 60 and 70 of us met each day to enjoy one another's company and share in activities. Some of their activities are among those listed on the following pages.

Make a start on the programme

One way of initial thinking is to group possible events in terms of:

- The "all-together" events (i.e., when there is something to watch or listen to or do together at the venue)
- The "small group" events
- The "off-site" events
- The "message giving" events

Some suggestions for these follow, from those who have gone before us!

The all-together sessions

A well-known visitor or Christian artist/dancer/singer/dramatist. Look under the section in the *UK Christian Handbook* called Musical and Theatrical Services. There are some talented Christians around, very hungry to be used!

Down Memory Lane. People bring things precious to them and are given three minutes to talk about them.

A "Brains Trust" with a panel. (A leaflet should be given out prior to this event to ask for questions.)

Music for everyone. This is a chance for everyone to join in by singing or playing an instrument. (One music teacher brought along a wide variety of instruments including keyboards.) How about a music quiz or perhaps a "music appreciation" session by a music lover?

Exercises ("chairobics") to music. (Comment: *"Hoots of laughter. Everyone relaxed."*)

Exhibitions of art, photography, flower arrangement, arts and crafts (perhaps the result of the "small-group" work).

Games. A large jigsaw is put on a table (*fit in three pieces before you leave*) and a giant Scrabble. Skittles. Indoor golf. Carpet bowls.

Competitions. How many Smarties in a jam jar? Who is that baby? (members bring photos of themselves as babies or children) and so on.

The "small group" sessions (or "workshops")

(If you don't fancy taking part, you can just watch. There'll be a chair!)

Sharing hobbies

Note: This – like the Brains Trust – needs ample preparation time. Scatter leaflets around the church saying something like:

If you have a hobby, would you be willing to talk about it to the holiday club? It could be done by question-and-answer with an interviewer if you feel nervous about standing up in front of a crowd by yourself.

Please complete the following and return it to us:

My hobby is. . . . .   Name . . . .

I am willing to talk about my hobby.

I would prefer to have an interviewer

I would need assistance to bring examples/equipment   Yes/No

Drama or play-reading (you don't have to learn lines!)
One group took the story of Ruth as their theme and the small group created a simple play based on the story of

Ruth which was then acted at the end of each day.

Cooking (even if you can't boil an egg!) Attempts included: a demonstration of how to cut and serve some of the more unusual fruits; breadmaking and buns; a snack in five minutes; marzipan flowers; the secret of curries.

Flower arranging (never done it before?) Various arrangements were demonstrated and guidance given about using unusual flower containers. Everyone had a go.

Keep fit (gentle – no trampolining) A physiotherapist led this session to music, using exercises designed for the elderly. This on several occasions has continued as a regular event.

Line dancing for beginners

The language of birds (by an enthusiast!)

Crafts. One group tried their skills at making batik pictures; another group drew a still-life arrangement. Others tried patchwork, tapestry, or painting on glass.

Here are another twenty ideas just to get you going: weaving, card-making, calligraphy for beginners, learning to draw, portrait painting, oil painting for beginners, framing pictures, how to sell what you write, flower painting in water-colours, Chinese brush painting, repairing and restoring furniture, working wood, painting miniatures, making a rag rug, silk painting, making embroidered boxes, hand-spinning, antique furniture and how to recognize it, wine tasting, getting the best from your camera, introduction to a PC.

The off-site events (two examples)

- We started one day with a morning walk (three "energy-levels"!) that met at a pub, followed by a conducted tour of a nearby church. Once the lunch was a barbecue in a neighbour's garden.
- In perfect weather we visited Waterperry Gardens near Oxford on a Thursday afternoon and had a time of blessed sunshine and flowers amidst the peace of the tree-lined gardens.

. . . and the gospel message?

We need to be frank about this. We do want our Christian message to be "spoken" clearly in some form as well as lived out, but on the other hand, this is not a time for sermons.

Very often the message is genuinely in the event itself: the friends that are made, the conversations that take place, the later absorption into a housegroup or something similar. But it is often good to have a "thought" to carry away, such as the story of Ruth, referred to previously, or a word of testimony from someone. But try not to let it look like the "religious bit" tagged on at the end. It needs to fit into the mood of the day and rest lightly on the landscape.

Here is how some "got the gospel in"!

- We always began with a "thought for the day" based on a song from a well-known musical.
- Because our theme had been summer holidays in general, we had a sort of "beach mission" ending when a London City Missioner came with members of the

Church Brownie Pack at the end of the last day. He gave a very challenging message (to us all), and we ended up with ice-cream cones!

- Each day one of our church members had spoken briefly about Jonah, the rebellious prophet. On our final day, Sunday, the play-reading group presented his story in the style of a Greek chorus, and we had invited a really good visiting speaker who showed how the power and wonder of God's forgiveness was revealed in Jesus.
- We finished with a thanksgiving and praise service in the church. It was a good idea, specially for the non churchgoers. The holiday club had been held a little distance from the main church, so this got them used to the church building in an atmosphere of welcome with friends already there. Various members spoke of what they had gained from the time together.
- Our final session was on the Sunday afternoon, when we had a special "Songs of Praise" in the church and invited the general congregation to join us. It was followed by tea. It was a very happy afternoon with a good number of those who had attended joining in.
- On the Sunday there was a special service in the village hall to which people could bring family and friends, and various things from the Holiday at Home were on display.

A quick note on publicity

Good publicity in good time is essential, but remember that even when we have sent out or given out hundreds of leaflets, we will end up with a rather smaller audience than we expected. But – if we have done our part faithfully – those are the people God has allowed us. Don't be too influenced by numbers. One of the most effective events I have heard of had sixteen participants.

Make use of posters. The CPO[1] have attractive posters, cards, and leaflets that can be overprinted with your own wording. Or get on to the computer-literate gang in the church who will probably do a good job for you.

Don't forget about the local radio station(s). Tell them in good time and you may be offered an interview. Get on to the local press. This is not for self-glory. All publicity for this is good publicity. Not all churches think that much about their elderly members.

And what happens when it's over?

Here are comments from those who have experienced the end as well as the beginning:

One lady phoned me immediately afterwards to thank me and she said, "There's never been anything like it in the parish before! I've never laughed so much in my life!" Older people met each other (instead of just their lunch club friends) and found new friends, new abilities and a new interest in church and in God. One lady had years ago acted in the local drama group and had become almost senile. But she threw herself into the drama and said afterwards, "It all came back!" I'm so glad we had the courage to do it.

Our Holiday at Home did not end on the last day. Eleven members came to the Sunday evening service, and everyone in the congregation was invited to look at the photos, the banner we made and the "Art Exhibition".

The event had been enjoyed and appreciated by everyone. Approximately 70 people had come. In general we felt that good friendships had been made there, and we had an increased respect for the skills of some of our members. We believe some have grown closer to the Lord, and an interest has been awakened in others.

And finally . . . the small white cloud . . . (1 Kings 18.44)

Of course it had been hard work. Many, many people were praying, and now we somehow have to keep up all the friendships which have been made. But we know this work has a special urgency about it. Within a few months of the end of our Holiday at Home two members had died in hospital. It reminded us that this work involves people who may be very near the end of their lives, and it could be, for some of them, their last chance to hear about the way of salvation, or to renew promises which they had once made.

In spite of our earlier hesitation and, I must admit, some disappointment that so few had enrolled, we had a really good time. We had learnt a lot about reflecting the love of God to strangers and about working together as a team of very assorted Christians, and the members of the church had stood with us in prayer throughout and did a great deal to help.

The real trouble started when the week ended and our new friends said "But what shall we do next week?" Really we felt we needed a six-week break in the Bahamas to recover, but we said we'd think about it. Eventually we felt it right to offer an Alpha course, and immediately began to wonder if there would be any response. The numbers, previously small, were now even smaller.

However, we pressed on. The few left had started to come to church regularly and brought some friends with them. This visible evidence of our little group encouraged some of the faithful old church members who had been praying for us, and they urged us to offer the Alpha course, even saying they would like to come. So even though we were so few in number, there really was no turning back. It was like Elijah seeing a small white cloud in the sky . . .

Now we are talking about the "next Alpha course" and whether the present one should now become a little "home group". So what is God going to do next? It is good he can still surprise us!

Material from: Juanita Kirby (Christ Church, Bromley, Kent); Ann Lear (St John the Baptist, Godalming, Surrey); Pat Gill (St Luke's, Whitfield, Glossop); Stan and Nancy Hornsby (Emmanuel Baptist Church, Swanage); Ron and Hazel Wilcox (St Leonards, Chesham Bois)

Possible titles for a Holiday at Home:

Celebrate Age
A New Outlook
On Line with God
An Upside-Down World (How do we hold on?)
Dreams and Visions
Heavens Above!
World's Apart: or are we?
Powering up
Health and Healing
New Stones for New Giants

CHAPTER EIGHT

"AND TODAY WE ARE HAPPY TO WELCOME . . ."

I remember a Rector some time back addressing his curate and other lay-preachers in his sitting room and asking us to respond to the question: What makes a good sermon? Everyone gave all the "right answers": biblically based, main points clear, good illustrations and so on. When it got to me, I lost a few Brownie points by saying, "One that is listened to".

The best sermon in the world is useless if people switch off.

I must be the classic non-listener. If I were really honest I would say that there are a few Christian speakers I could listen to for hours, but for the most part I have, over the years, missed a large part of all church sermons. I do hope I am an exception.

I can remember raising this matter with a class of young pastors in Kenya who got very indignant about it. "Whose fault is it, if people don't listen to you?" I had asked. "Well, it's theirs," they replied at once. "It's their duty to listen." We talked it over and they began to see what I meant. "Duty" or not, ordinary people listen to what affects them, what interests them, what their daily life is about, where their struggles and problems are. If you talk only about what affects and interests you, they are likely to turn off quite soon.

And according to a well-known percentage rate, they will only benefit from 20% of what they hear, anyway. So let's take it from there.

There are, of course, many different Christian meetings we might get involved in: the "Over-60s fellowship", "Senior seekers", "Prime Time" and so on. Then there are many Christian organizations, too many to list here, who are always in search of good speakers. Subjects you can be asked to speak on can be factual, creative, educational, of general interest, life experiences and so on.

I suspect most of you reading this will be involved in some such meeting and are always searching desperately for new topics and new speakers that will interest your members. This chapter, however, assumes you are going to be the speaker and want to speak on the Christian faith and what it means.

Just how do we "preach" the gospel of Jesus to a fairly uninterested group of older people sitting in chairs in a rather depressing hall? Some may be churchgoers (but you suspect they could do with some help). Others just frankly are not especially interested and go to sleep at this point.

It is perhaps significant that, as I dig back into my memories, the "talks" I remember at countless "ladies' fellowships" were not concerned with spiritual matters. In the more immediate past, I remember two. One was

"Maggie" describing her daughter's wedding, and the other was "Stella" telling us about her holiday in Crete.

Strange really, because they don't sound great subjects, do they? In fact, on the whole, to be avoided. ("So next week, we'll all be glad to welcome Mrs Palmer, who will be showing us her slides of her holiday in Cornwall.") So why do I remember them?

They – both – made us laugh. Maggie included the reality of spending days searching London for a wedding dress and ending up buying it in Luton, and of trying to set up wedding photos when a horse-drawn carriage taking tourists around kept getting in the picture. Stella brought the problems of unfamiliarity in a different culture vividly to mind. Calamity seemed to follow calamity as she and her husband tried to get the right boat to the right place at the right time and ended up in a police station.

You see, we identified with what they were saying. It happens. Things don't always go right in our normal lives for anyone. Sometimes we are forced either to laugh or cry, and both Maggie and Stella were managing the laughter, now it was all over.

Suggestion 1: Use personal experiences. People are interested in people.

Let's relax as we give a talk. Let's give the impression that being a Christian is more than going to church. It's trying to live by the standards Christ has set. It means there's another driver in the car to whom we must listen, and that might land us in difficulties. Bring the Christian faith alive: into shopping, working, visiting the doctor, dealing with your teenage son, getting up on time (or not), and so on. Start where they are.

And don't pretend things don't go wrong.

A friend, a husband dies. Your daughter-in-law is diagnosed with multiple sclerosis. You yourself recognize arthritis is going to cripple you shortly. We don't leap around laughing at that. We try to work it through. Everyone has to. The only difference (and it's a big one) is that for us, Christ is by our side. Talk about how he helps.

So that's one sort of talk: a "real" testimony of your (ordinary) life with Jesus, an honest selection of the good, the bad, and the indifferent of your walk with him. You might at the end give the message: Jesus is alive and with us all the way.

Suggestion 2: Help them to see the place and value of old age in the wider scheme of creation. For example:

Centre your thoughts on the picture of life and death shown in the concept of the morning and the evening. When people come home from work, what can the evening offer them? Relaxation, absence of stress, people you love, food you choose, rest when you need it, and so on. Write some of them on a flip chart. Can that be related to old age?

Remember that the Jewish Sabbath starts in the evening. (In Genesis 1 and 2 each act of creation is concluded with the words: ". . . and the evening and the morning was the first day" . . . and so on.) Talk a little about the Jewish concept of the day which begins as we go to bed, not exhausted at the "end of the day", but a beginning for God. Nothing stops at night. The moon continues to circle the earth, the seeds push up their way as spring arrives, the rivers flow, the creatures hunt in the forest. Life goes on, and when we wake we are ready to move into a day already begun by God. Think it through.

What about the actual seasons as they pass? We may talk about a new life ahead as the seeds drop from the dead trees into the ground. Can we teach a special way to take a walk where we see, and feel, and touch, and smell and hear as we were taught as children and now have forgotten?

Suggestion 3: Teach what the Bible has to say about old age.

One way to present this is to speak on "Spiritual Arthritis", which is what we suffer from when our spiritual lives become stiff and inactive, despite Paul's words in 2 Cor. 4.16 that "though outwardly we are wasting away, yet inwardly we are being renewed day by day". Speak on the temptations all of us experience in later years: to drop into the slow lane spiritually, to join our friends in a constant round of complaint, to be demoralized by the attitudes of others, to give in to fear of the future. Then study the spiritual armour in Ephesians 6 and apply them to daily living as an older Christian in today's society.

Suggestion 4: How dark is your sky? Think about darkness, its good and its danger. We see so many more things when the sky is black and only the moon reflects the light of the sun. In the orange sky of the cities and towns, so much is missing. What, in our lives, becomes clearer, more precious in times of trouble? Then what of the "watchmen that wait for the morning" (Psalm 130.5–6)? We too, in the winter, wait eagerly for the first light of dawn. Do we wait, like that, for the Lord's return and, having confidence that the time will come, perhaps sometimes use these words found written on the walls of a cellar in Cologne, Germany, after World War 2?

I believe in the sun even when it is not shining,
I believe in Love when I feel it not
I believe in God even when he is silent.

Is that true of you?

Suggestion 5: What about the positives concerning old age?

Consider the book of memories we have. Would you really like to start all over again? Are there some pages we want to tear out?

We are out of the rat race, the anxieties of today. The fight for position, for recognition, or success is over.

We are on the way home. Do we really feel that?

Maybe none of the above thoughts appeal, but they are based on the need to encourage older people into the Kingdom, and help them to see life and death as things to accept without fear.

God bless you as you do it.

CHAPTER NINE

LOTS OF LOVELY IDEAS

It is generally accepted that all Christians should be witnesses for Christ. Jesus told us to go to Jerusalem, Samaria, and then the world. For many of us in later years it is often "Jerusalem" that is the difficulty: to witness to our friends, our neighbours, the people we get to know by meeting them regularly in the post office or at the Horticultural society or in the local library.

"We should make sure," wrote the Director of Spearhead Mission in Bolton,[1] "that any strategy for evangelism starts with reaching the individual for Christ: going to them in their own environments and need."

So this is a chapter of "conversation starters" with older people, just to give you an idea or two about making and developing contacts. They are built around a well known song from *The King and I*:

Getting to know you . . .

I'm the Neighbourhood watch representative. I hope you don't mind my mentioning you really shouldn't leave your kitchen window open when you go out.

I'm sorry. It's tapioca again. I know you hate it. I'll see if they've got something else next time. (Meals on Wheels)

If I've counted the number of times this bus is late . . . and always when it's raining!

Look, it says there's a walk around the village on Saturday with Mr Diver. You know: he's a local historian. I don't really like going alone. How about going together?

Have you seen that film about dinosaurs yet? Everyone's talking about it. How about trying it out? (This relates to any special event you might go to together: a talked-about film is a good starter. Not many older people get to recently released films.)

We've got a coach going from the church to the Coast Railway/National Trust Exhibition/Prince of Wales Theatre/ Trooping of the Colour . . . How about joining us?

I have to go to the Garden Centre tomorrow. Would you like to come with me? You get a good cup of coffee there.

Getting to know all about you . . .

You're fond of music, aren't you? There's a good concert next week . . .

I rather like a Sunday lunch at the pub sometimes. Saves me cooking. Were you thinking of coming to church? We could go along together afterwards.

I'm tired of playing Scrabble with my friend down the street! She's got that dreadful list of two-letter words no one has ever heard of. Do you play?

I didn't realize you were needing treatment at the hospital. Why don't I take you there this time? I've a friend there I'd like to visit.

We've got a sort of special event at the church on Saturday. I think you'd enjoy it.

Getting to like you . . .

How about joining the bowls club? They're always looking for members.

Can I come to that Seniors club with you? It sounds fun.

I'm thinking I'll start planning a regular tea-party or coffee-morning at home this winter. I don't like being alone in the house all the time. "Muffin mornings" or "p.m. pancakes". What do you think?

Do come next Tuesday. We're making Christmas centre-pieces, Janet's ever so good at it and then Tom (you know, that cheery cockney plumber) is going to tell us how near he felt to God during times of danger in the forces.

So glad you're coming to church now and again. Are you any good at designing cards: perhaps for the bereaved or those in trouble that we know of? There's a group on a Friday afternoon in the church rooms having some difficulty with finding enough help.

Did you know they've started holding a Church "Home group" in the morning now? I was thinking of going. Shall we go together for the first one?

. . . Getting to hope you like me

I've been thinking. Could we organize a walk for older people from the Village on the Bank Holiday coming? We could have three different "levels" but all end up at that pub near the Golf Course.

Did you know there's a special weekend at the church next month, just for seniors? It's called a "Holiday at Home". Can I show you the programme?

I was wondering if you could help me. You see the Pastor's sermon is going to be recorded on tape and we can take one to anyone who can't get to church these days. I was thinking those two ladies in the Nursing Home we visit would love them. How about coming with me and suggesting it to them?

Oh, and I've just seen a really good video. How about coming around and we'll watch it together. It's introducing that Alpha course they're all talking about.

And with the housebound?

Getting to know you, Getting to feel free and easy . . .

I've been asked by the social services to call on you some-times: just to see how you're doing. No, I didn't have any-thing special to offer but I'd love a cup of tea.

I hear your dog needs a walk now and again. I need to lose a few pounds, can I help out? I live down West Street.

When is it you have to go in for the operation? I'll try and visit on Saturday.

. . . When I am with you, getting to know what to say . . .

You know, I really enjoy coming here. It's so peaceful. Is that a picture of your grandchildren?

I brought you some pictures of my family. This is the little daughter we lost in a car accident. One never really forgets, do you?

Yes, well families so often move around these days. Still, that's a card from them, isn't it? More than I get from my brother!

By the way, I wondered if you'd like this large-print New Testament? I remember you saying you used to go to church.

It's Easter Sunday quite soon. There's a service on the TV, isn't there? Could I come and watch it with you? Your TV's much bigger than mine.

I brought a tape with me today . . . I wondered if you'd like it . . .

And the song ends:

> Haven't you noticed?
> Suddenly I'm bright and easy
> Because of all the beautiful and new
> Things I'm learning about you
> Day by day!

CHAPTER TEN

YES, IT DOES HAPPEN!

Testimonies from those who found Christ in later years.

At an evangelistic meeting

Mildred French (Southsea, Hampshire, UK) was 53 and very much under the impression she was a Christian. She and her husband even went to church occasionally. In November 1985 her married daughter urged them to go to a "Down to Earth" mission held on Southsea Common.

Her words follow:

For an Anglican it was a real culture shock. I hated it but when the speaker said the prayer of commitment I found myself joining in. When I finished, a feeling of great warmth and peace filled me. I didn't "go up to the front" but life – and I – changed a good deal after that. My husband also came to Jesus some weeks later and we pray and work together now.

At home or through a family member

Janet Kraske (Bowthorpe, Norfolk, UK):

> About two years after my father's death my mother decided to come and stay for the weekend as it was my son's birthday. I had a meeting to attend and it was difficult to postpone it, so I left Mum for an hour on her own. When I got back she was in tears. I was full of apology thinking it was because she had been left on her own, but it turned out she had read some gospel tracts I had in the lounge and wanted to give her life to the Lord. We spent a wonderful time and I led her into a prayer of commitment. Sadly she is no longer with us, but the last few years of her life were the happiest.

Mary Matthews (Northampton, UK):

> I went to Sunday School when I was a child and kept going fairly regularly to church although I often thought, "Why do I come here?" However, most of my friends were there so I kept going. Then my children began to leave home and I began to feel rather empty inside. Harold and I seemed to be going different ways, and I started taking prescribed Valium.
>
> Then I was washing up after Sunday lunch one afternoon, and my younger son who had come home from college came into the kitchen and said, "Can I help you, Mum?"
>
> Well, my children didn't do things like that! I'd got

fed up asking. I thought, "That's funny. There's something different about you."

Well, he kept piling Christian books on me, book after book, and I read them all. One had a commitment prayer in it, and I prayed that prayer alone in the living room and didn't think much more about it. Then about three weeks later I felt the Lord's presence very strongly in a way I had never felt before. I think that's where it all started.

From Willa Syratt (Puckeridge, Hertfordshire, UK). Jim, with no religious background, had married a Christian girl after the war. They "rubbed along" (his words) with different views for many years, "during which I was introduced to grace at meals and my wife going to church". When he was about 60, his wife broke her ankle and wasn't able to manage the steps at church. Jim explained, "I wasn't going to let anyone else carry her up the steps so I started going with her." He listened to a few sermons and began to think about Jesus and his life. So, when he was invited by the minister to attend a "seekers" class with three other unbelievers "who like me loved to argue about every little details of the Christian message", he agreed. Gradually he heard and accepted the message of Jesus and was baptized within a year. He says: "Since accepting him as my Saviour I have experienced a peace that was unknown before."

From Grace Jacobs (Emsworth, Hampshire, UK). Mr B, a professional man, lived in northwest India. Although he was a Hindu he had married an English lady and went to church in India with her and the children. When he retired they came to England, where his wife became ill. Home communion on request was brought from the church, and Mr B always stayed in the room for the short service. When his wife died he asked to be baptized and confirmed, showing signs of real faith.

In hospital

From Jill Lawson (Sevenoaks, Kent, UK). Betty was dying of lung cancer at the age of 63. Her Christian sister asked a clergyman to call who had known her sister in early days. He introduced himself and showed Betty a card with a cross on it and the words JESUS DIED FOR MEN.

"Do you believe that, Betty?" he asked. She said she did and then he took a pen and crossed out one letter. The N.

"Do you know that means you?" he said, and was able to explain further and led her in a prayer of commitment.

At a residential home

From Jill Lawson (Sevenoaks, Kent, UK). Tilly was a resident at a retirement home that I visit. With encouragement she began to attend the monthly communion service. On one occasion she was in tears throughout and blurted out that she was a wicked woman.

"What makes you say that?" I asked, and she told me a story of so hating her mother because she favoured her sister that she had refused to go to her funeral. This had preyed on her mind ever since.

We talked about repentance and the grace and forgiveness of God and about how we needed to accept what God was longing to offer us.

"If I brought you a bunch of flowers, Tilly," I said, "you could either find a jar and arrange them nicely and enjoy them, or you could throw them on the floor and trample them."

"Oh, I wouldn't do that," she assured me, and I knew she understood. Tilly died a few months later, but I believe the living God met with her that day.

From Dorothy Brooks (Sheffield, Yorkshire, UK) "Elsie" speaks for herself:

I have not had a good life, having been an alcoholic for years and living a completely immoral life. For a while I became a Mormon in my search for God. Then I came to this residential home and found that Christians visited, telling of Jesus and his love and compassion. I really wanted to know more. I seriously asked God to tell me which was right, Mormonism or the God of the Christians. Two days later there was a carol service at the home and the lady was speaking about the real meaning of joy, when suddenly the Lord Jesus came to me and filled me with incredible joy. Afterwards the Christians laid hands on me and prayed for a headache I had had for a month. It disappeared and hasn't returned. The Lord came to me, filled me with joy and forgave my sin. Jesus truly is the Way, the Truth and the Life.

Listening to a tape

From Doreen Crowe (Tonbridge, Kent, UK). A lady in her late 70s walked into our church office to ask if she could join our Keep Fit group. She also learned to play badminton. She began to come to church. I gave her Steve Chalke's tape. She said that there were a few things on the tape she did not understand, so we listened to the tape together. Now, with a fresh understanding, she committed her life to the Lord, attended an Alpha course and was baptized. We also invite folk at our church luncheon club to take the Jesus video home with them. Two ladies of those who did expressed a wish to learn more about Jesus. This Easter Sunday (2000) one of those ladies, aged 87, is being baptized.

Invited to a church meeting

From Grace Jacobs (Emsworth, Hampshire, UK). Charles was invited to our monthly meetings by a friend. He was not living near but, dressed smartly in a navy pinstripe suit, came by bus every month for two years, listening but never responding to anything on a spiritual level. He then, sadly, had a serious stroke, and I was able to visit him in hospital and pray with him. Transferred to a nursing home, through the ministry of a relative he received the Lord into his life. He now spends his days praying for the other residents of the nursing home and writing wobbly letters with his left hand (because of the stroke) praising God for his goodness, and asking prayer for the needy around him.

CHAPTER ELEVEN

DRAMA FOR ALL

Drama is usually appreciated, and good professional groups performing for your over-55s group will be welcomed by them. The suggestions that follow, however, are for ordinary members of your over-55s group and should be easily performed by those interested. Such small dramas are often easier to listen to than a talk, and they make the point more forcibly. Many can be written or thought up by the actors themselves without too much difficulty.

Points to remember

Actors must be heard, and some of your audience may be hard of hearing. So what do you do?

If your audience is a small one, then you may be able to speak slowly and loudly enough to be heard. However, nag at the people who either talk too quickly or who drop their voices at the ends of sentences.

If the audience is larger, use the microphones. I often hear older people say, "Oh, I don't like those radio mikes" but, if you have them, use them. It is essential that you are heard. How often I have seen performances in which I have heard less than half of what is going on.

If you only have fixed mikes, then clearly you can't do too much moving around, but often plays can be read at the mike like radio plays. Since you probably don't have stage lighting, this is often an acceptable way of doing it anyway, as words are heard where actions might be unseen.

Where do you find a script?

Books of readings or short plays with a Christian message are obtainable at Christian bookshops (although they do go out of print fairly rapidly). However, I have not yet found one that has older people specially in mind. So it often comes back to us. Here are some suggested ideas that might encourage you either to write your own script or simply to "ad lib". It's not as difficult as all that!

Some plays lend themselves to making up the words more or less as you go along. Unsurprisingly, the parables of Jesus can be offered like this. Suggestions on acting out four parables follow:

Examples of dramatizing parables

The Pearl (Matthew 13.45–46). The Bible says: "The kingdom of heaven is like a merchant looking for fine pearls. When he found one of great value, he went away and sold everything he had and bought it." That's all there is, but it's a good story.

The acting needs three people: the merchant, his wife, and the trader who is selling.

Scene 1: The merchant sees the pearl (he is a buyer so pretends not to be interested, etc.) The trader is only too aware of the buyer's interest. Price bargaining begins (don't drag it out). In the end the merchant persuades the trader to let him take it home to show his wife (since the price is so high). Unlikely, I know, but indicate that the trader knows the merchant well and trusts him.

Scene 2: The merchant, now at home, begins gradually to prepare his wife for what he has to tell her: that everything is going to be sold to buy this pearl. This is humorous. He is afraid to admit he wants to sell everything. It proceeds from, "Do we need such a big TV?" to "Do we really *need* a car? Isn't this house getting a little big for us?" And so on. The wife gets more and more upset. "Are you in debt? You've bought a new car!" etc. In the end he confesses what he has done and shows her the pearl. Wife is stunned at its beauty. The merchant says something like, "Isn't that worth all we have?" and she agrees.

Taking part in a drama can teach powerful things. I was part of acting this one out in a conference workshop once. I was the "merchant" and in Scene 1 just could not agree on the price with the older lady playing the part of the trader. Everything I offered she refused. The audience got a bit restless. In the end I hissed: "You've got to sell it to me. We're holding things up!" It was just a funny episode to us, and the "trader" laughed and apologized afterwards. But what stuck in my mind was that lady telling the story from the conference platform on the last night when people were asked to share any special blessing during the time. "I realized then, as never before, how precious the Kingdom of God; is to me," she said. "I just couldn't let it go."

The Good Samaritan (Luke 10.30–37).

This can be done with two people, a screen (for the hat-change to take place) a post with BUS STOP on it and a notice of sorts, and a few hats.

An older person is at a bus stop trying to read the bus timetable and is very worried. The other actor changes his hat several times behind the screen and is, in turn, (a) the local Vicar; (b) an official of some type (depends what hat you have!); (c) a young football fan with scarf, shirt, rattle – whatever – who does stop and help her.

The Lost Coin (Luke 15.8–10). Just think of something valuable. Dressing for a wedding, perhaps, and an earring is lost, or a brooch belonging to someone else. You "can't go without it". Disaster! Or it could be the car keys that you desperately need? Do we feel like that about winning people for Jesus?!

The Unmerciful Servant (Matthew 18.23–35). Perhaps it's a window cleaner who bought a car from a friend who has just let him off the last £500 (which he can't manage). Then the cleaner is furious at an old lady who can't pay him the £4 needed for the window he's just cleaned.

And so on.

Ideas from our daily experiences

But it doesn't have to be a parable. Here are some other ideas for small plays from our daily experiences that would not be too difficult to act successfully without having to learn a specific script.

The following idea originated with a small group of older ladies in Weston-super-Mare, UK. It was intended for Christmas, although it can be adapted.

THE THREE PRESENTS

Message: the Christian faith is not (a) something quite private and not to be talked about, or (b) old-fashioned, irrelevant and dull. But it is (c) something given freely by God who knows our needs and loves us.

Three older people have decided to spend Christmas evening together and have kept a present each to open together. They open them in turn.

PERSON 1: Unwraps a good piece of jewellery. There is a lot of teasing. Is it from someone at the lunch club? A secret admirer or similar? She tries it on but won't wear it. It is too precious and perhaps would embarrass her. She says she will keep it safe under lock and key or in the bank and puts it carefully back in the box.

PERSON 2 (can be a man): Unwraps a garment knitted by an older sister/aunt who has arthritic hands and is always knitting for someone. The recipient doesn't like it and holds it up to ridicule. He/she is tired of getting garments like this. He puts it aside, unwanted. The others rebuke him, saying it cost the one who made it care and effort and she did it out of love.

PERSON 3: Her husband is abroad and she knows he will have sent her something she really wants and needs because he knows her and loves her. She unwraps the gift (a coffee pot or similar) and is delighted and proceeds to use it at once.

Then one by one the three stand up and explain that people treat the gift of God in these three ways.

THE WAY WE SEE THINGS

A Christian visits two ladies saying the same thing to both, and getting totally different responses. Message: Our general attitude to life can greatly contribute to our happiness.

(Knock at door)

MRS GREEN   *(Grumbling)* Oh goodness me! No peace these days. Who on earth is visiting me now? If they're collecting for something again . . . ! *(Opens door)*

MRS WHITE   Hello, Mrs Green. I'm Mrs White from across the road. We moved in last week. I've been thinking I'd like to get acquainted with people around. May I come in for a moment?

GREEN   I suppose you'd better. (*To cat*) You'll have to get off your chair, Ruby. Come on darling, just for a minute.

WHITE   (*Sitting down*) I saw you sitting in the window. What a lovely outlook you have. You can see all the children going to school and people taking their dogs for a walk. There's a lovely Labrador who belongs to that gentleman in the next street.

GREEN   (*Interrupting*) Dogs! Don't mention them. Every one of them stops at my gate. You watch this one . . . There you are! And as for children. The noise they make! You want to be here when the street has about 50 cars in it picking them up. And as for the window, it's a wonder I can see anything at all. I haven't seen that man that calls himself a window-cleaner for weeks.

. . . and so on. Contrast it with Mrs White going to visit Mrs Brown next door, using the same conversation but getting totally different answers. You need to keep the audience laughing for the first one and friendly towards the second.

THE WASHING MACHINE

Message: If we don't want to hear something, we will manage not to. This presents humorously our tendency to delay things and can be linked with our delay to take Jesus seriously or get involved with church.

Presenter announces loudly the days of the week, or has someone carry a large card around to indicate the change of days.

Monday

ANNIE There's your coffee, dear. Got some of those biscuits you like, too.

BERT (*Reading paper*) Oh that's great (*stretching out hand without looking*). Thanks.

ANNIE Those roses have done really well this year, haven't they? That's the way you cut them back in September . . . you've got a real gift for it.

BERT Hmmm . . .

ANNIE Oh by the way, dear. There's something wrong with the washing machine . . . I wonder if you'd just look at it for me . . . It – er – well it flooded the floor when you were out this morning. Took ages to clear up.

BERT Oh . . . yes. I'll see to it . . .

ANNIE Thank you, dear.

Tuesday

(*Annie is folding something on a chair . . . Bert passes, obviously going out.*)

ANNIE Oh . . . are you going out, this morning, Bert?

BERT Yes . . . you know I said to Mrs Bennet I'd have a look at her shed roof for her. It was letting in rain she said . . .

ANNIE   (*A bit disconcerted*) Oh ... I was hoping you'd have time to look at the washing machine. You remember I told you yesterday it wasn't working properly.

BERT   Oh did you? I'd forgotten. I'll see to it later.

Wednesday

ANNIE   (*On phone*) Well, we've had it a good many years I know but it isn't that we use it all the time. (*Pause*) No I can't wait until next month! We have visitors coming next week! (*Pause. Sees Bert passing.*) Yes, we fixed it last time but my husband's rather busy just now ... Well please do your best!
(*Bert has disappeared. She calls after him . . .*) Bert! BERT!

Thursday

BERT   (*Coming into the kitchen*) Hey, there's water on the floor here, Annie. Did you know?

ANNIE   Bert, I've been telling you all week about the washing machine. I tried to fix it myself, but it still seems to be leaking.

BERT   (*In good humour. Laughs*) My dear! When did you learn how to mend electrical things? Leave it to me. It probably just needs a new hose or something. I've got something that will do in the shed.

ANNIE   Yes, but if you could do it soon ...

BERT   Of course I will, dearest. When I get back from bowls. Did I tell you my score last week? I've really got to do better today.

Friday

BERT   Annie! ANNIE! Where's my best shirt? You know it's the ramblers' club committee this morning.

ANNIE   It's on the radiator! You know I had to hand wash everything last night and it just isn't dry yet.

BERT   What do you mean "hand wash"? Put it in the machine!

ANNIE   The machine is *out of order*, Bert. It has been all week. I've been telling you every day.

BERT   Well what do I do about my shirt?

ANNIE   You'll have to wear another. I'll get you one, but PLEASE will you see to it tomorrow?

Saturday

ANNIE   (*On phone*) Yes, that'll be lovely, dear. You'll bring all the family, won't you? (*Pause*) Oh yes, Father will be here. We love you coming, you know that.

BERT   (*Coming in*) Oh, what's that? John and Marion coming over?

ANNIE   Yes . . . and the children. They'll be here about three o'clock. That will give you time to . . .

BERT   (*Excited*) Oh, I'll get the train set out again and put it in the dining room. You know, Christopher's just getting to the age when he'll love it.

ANNIE   You mean YOU love it. But – honestly, Bert – there's a huge stack of washing . . . (*but he has gone*).

Sunday

BERT   (*Calling*) You ready for church, Annie?

ANNIE   (*Angry*) No, I'm not. I haven't got anything to wear and I've got to clean up after yesterday. I still haven't got the washing machine mended!!

BERT   Well, you can hardly expect me to do it on a Sunday. It's a day of rest. I'll see to it on Monday. Come along, do. We'll be late.

There is endless scope for laughing at ourselves but learning while we do it.

What happened then?

Some largely impromptu plays can centre on a well-known Bible story. They will need some scripting but not necessarily line-by-line learning. Take a well-known Bible story and have the characters in it discuss what has happened as if it is today. It can be a way to bring the stories alive. For example:

The shepherds (Luke 2.8) try to tell their friends about the vision in the fields and what happened then, and get asked what they have been drinking.

A soldier of Israel who missed the David and Goliath event because he was on leave hears all about it from excited friends.

A discussion takes place between two friends about this man Noah who insists on building an ark. Ending remark something like: "Blimey, this rain's really getting me down! Let's go and have a pint."

A television news reporter who only just escaped tries to persuade his boss in Jerusalem to run the story of Samson and the Temple of Dagon in Gaza.

Oh when the saints . . .

Dramatized interviews with a heavenly gatekeeper can show many people's explanations of why they should get in and the gatekeeper's reply to their justification.

Drama can also be used in training

What do I say when . . . ?

There are many things commonly said by older people to Christians who are trying to talk to them about Jesus. The five vignettes that follow show two older ladies (a bit nervous) who are committed to evangelizing and ready to attempt it in different situations. The vignettes deliberately stop when the "awkward response" is given (a bell or something similar could ring) and the two would-be evangelists find themselves not sure what to say. A discussion could then take place with the audience as to what sort of reply could be given. You could make a collection of the suggested responses.

The actors should speak the turn-off sentences loudly and clearly. Each time the key-line is spoken, all actors should "freeze" for a moment or two to indicate that the "play" is ended. The key-line can be repeated or put on the overhead while discussion takes place. Offered responses can be written on the overhead. Perhaps other "turn-off phrases" can be suggested.

SCENE ONE: IN THE SHOP

MARY   So where are we going first?

JOAN   How about the shop? Sheila helps out this afternoon, and I've been longing to ask her why she
and Bill never come to church now that they're
retired. I need some milk anyway.

MARY   Well, you do it. I'll look around the shelves and
pray for you. (*Pause*)

JOAN   Just a pint of semi-skimmed please, dear.

SHEILA   Here you are, then. Keeping well are you?

JOAN   Yes. How are the family?

SHEILA   Oh they're doing fine. Enjoying the shop very
much. Bill and I like having more time to ourselves as well.

JOAN   (*Leaping into the opportunity given*) I thought
perhaps we'd see you at church now that you've
got a bit more time.

SHEILA   Oh, we've never been much of a family for
churchgoing. Too much else to do, really, on a
Sunday.

JOAN   But don't you ever feel you need to believe in
something beyond this world? Have some kind
of faith in God?

SHEILA   Oh I believe in a God somewhere . . . say my
prayers sometimes, too. That's good enough for
me.

SCENE TWO: IN THE HOME

JOAN   I really feel I must say something to Mrs Long today, Mary. I've been visiting her for so long and never really got Jesus into the conversation.

MARY   All right. Shall I come with you?

JOAN   No, she'd only wonder why. You know, she's always so suspicious. Just pray for me. (*Pause*)

JOAN   Mrs Long, there's something I've been meaning to talk to you about.

MRS L   Huh! Your religious bit, is it? I thought you'd get there. All the same, you church people.

JOAN   I'm only mentioning it because you so often say you're lonely. You know, God really helps me not to feel so alone now that I've lost my husband. Whether you believe in him or not, God is there, loving us, and wanting us to belong to his family.

MRS L   Look at the way the world is today. All that killing, all the children dying of disease and starvation. If there's a God in charge of this, he's no God of love!

SCENE THREE: IN THE RESIDENTIAL HOME

MARY   Let's go together to Good Havens this afternoon, Joan. After the minister's left, we can really spend a little time with the old people. You know he has to get back for the meeting with the General Purposes Committee today.

JOAN   All right. I think it's so bad to look hurried all the
        time. I've specially been praying for Mrs Wilson
        lately. She looks so unhappy and cross.

JOAN   Hello, Mrs Wilson. Did you enjoy the service?

MRS W   Eh?

JOAN   Did you like the hymns we sang?

MRS W   What all about "Tell Me the Old, Old Story"? Not
        much in that for me in this state, is there?

JOAN   I think there's a lot, if you're in pain. That last one
        was all about God helping us in trouble.

MRS W   Well, he's not helping me much, is he? It's all right
        for you. You can go anywhere you want. You
        wouldn't talk about God in here with all these
        stupid women around and with your leg giving
        you so much pain you can't even think! What's he
        got to do with this? There is no purpose in living
        on like this. I've been asking the doctor to give me
        something. No one would care!

SCENE FOUR: IN THE BUS

MARY   Hello, Helen. Can I sit with you?

HELEN   Yes, of course.

MARY   I've just been to a meeting with the Baptist church
        women's group. They seem to be a happy lot.

HELEN   What were you doing there? I thought you were
        Church of England.

MARY   I was speaking to them about how God helps us

in trouble. You know I enjoy doing that kind of thing.

HELEN   Oh yes . . . You go to church, don't you?

MARY   That's right. Don't you ever think about things like that?

HELEN   I think about it, yes, but it really doesn't bother me. After all, no one really knows the truth, do they? Most of the world's religions have good things and bad in them.

MARY   But don't you ever think about what will happen when you die?

HELEN   Well, I look at it like this. I didn't seem to have much choice about arriving in this life, so I might just as well take potluck in the next!

SCENE FIVE: AT THE DOORSTEP

MARY   You know, Joan, I'm not really very good at knocking on doors.

JOAN   I don't suppose anyone is really, but Christmas does give us a good excuse. After all, lots of people do come to church at Christmas.

MARY   Well, I'm glad we go together.

JOAN   They'll think we're Jehovah Witnesses! (*Knocking*)

Good evening. We're just calling from the local church to let you know about the services for Christmas.

WOMAN   Thanks. I'll see about it.

JOAN   Are you churchgoers?

WOMAN   Not now, I'm not. Not the way the church is
            today. It isn't the same as it used to be, with that
            young vicar with his lad on drugs and every-
            one clapping their hands and things. I was
            married in the church, mind, and I expect I'll be
            buried there. I went once, years ago, but I didn't
            know a single hymn! That's not what I call
            church.

Four-minute opportunities (Role-playing)

In the situations below, find one of the group willing to act
the person described. You (in the evangelizing role) feel
very strongly that this is an opportunity God has given
you to get across the gospel to this person. Those acting
the people being evangelized simply follow the leads.
They may reject, listen politely though quite uninterested,
think they are dealing with a lunatic, ask difficult questions or accept what is being said. The other members of
the group will be watching and will comment afterwards.
(Don't worry. They will be on your side!)

(1) Helen Barker is sitting in a hospital waiting room. It
is a cancer clinic and her husband, Colin, has just been
called to a consultation. They have recently retired and
live fairly comfortably in a private bungalow in a small
town nearby. They go to church at Christmas and have
usually kept their name on the electoral roll though as yet
haven't linked up with a local church. You find yourself
sitting by her and get into conversation.

(2) You usually take Kate Whitley into a shopping

complex on a Saturday and know her fairly well although don't see her alone much. She is a single retired nurse and has always been quite uninterested in spiritual things. Once you had asked her to church, and she said she was a Roman Catholic and there was no church near. One Saturday you are in your car with her waiting for a third friend to come out of the supermarket. You think, "This is my opportunity".

(3) William Morrison is 76 and you have called to tell him about a mobile library that is going to come to the area. He is a widower and an ex-farmer who drops down to the pub most nights. He has been in church about twice in his life but has the impression he belongs to it. Doesn't care for the local minister.

(4) Ellen Woods lives next door to you, although you hardly ever meet her. She is a widow with family living nearby and much involved in the problems of the family and helping with grandchildren, etc. She appears to have no interest whatsoever in Christianity. One day you get chatting with her outside the local post office.

Though we have primarily been trying to encourage you to provide your own scripts – someone around will have a gift for it! – we have included in the appendix to this chapter two scripts written by Outlook members.

Appendix

This includes two scripted plays, "Independent Harry" and "Where Are You?"

INDEPENDENT HARRY

A play by Stan and Nancy Hornsby. Message: We cannot manage alone.

This drama needs two readers (who narrate), and Harry, the main character, who can act alone or with an "extra", if available, who is able to mime the car, the train, the neighbour, and the guard.

ONE This is the story of Independent Harry.

TWO One day Harry had to go on his weekly visit to the Health Centre.

ONE He got to the bus stop.

TWO And as he waited, (*Friend enters driving car*)

ONE he saw a friend approaching in a car.

TWO (*Excitedly*) Thinking he might be offered a lift,

ONE (*Poshly*) he turned round and looked the other way.

TWO (*Poshly*) He preferred to be independent.

ONE (*Poshly*) He could cope perfectly well without help from anybody else. (*Friend drives off*)

TWO So he waited . . .

ONE . . . and waited . . .

TWO . . . and waited . . .

ONE . . . And then . . .

TWO . . . he waited some more.

ONE It then struck him that the buses might be on strike.

TWO Which was most unusual.

ONE He wondered what to do.

TWO Then he had to make a decision.

ONE He decided that . . . maybe he should walk.

TWO After a brief pause for further thought,

ONE he did just that.

TWO Eventually,

ONE he arrived at the Health Centre.

TWO Tired!

ONE Breathless!

TWO (*Sternly*) And late!

ONE Tut! Tut!

TWO If only he'd called out to his friend.

ONE He could have saved himself the wait,

TWO and the walk,

ONE and being late.

TWO (*Obstinately*) But he could look after himself. (*Pause*)

ONE The next week Harry had to go to the Health Centre again.

TWO Today, he would go by car. (*Gets into car*)

ONE Clunk.

TWO Click.

ONE He turned the key.

TWO Dudududududududu!

ONE And the engine roared into life.

TWO Then promptly cut out.

ONE Harry shrugged his shoulders,

TWO turned the key again,

ONE And the engine . . . didn't roar into life.

TWO In fact it just went . . .

ONE Click.

TWO Fifty-five clicks later,

ONE Harry felt depressed. (*Neighbour enters*)

TWO He got out of his car,

ONE And waved to his neighbour . . .

TWO (*Knowingly*) A mechanic.

ONE who had just stepped out of his house.

TWO Harry thought of asking for help.

ONE (*Poshly*) But quickly dismissed such a degrading idea.

TWO (*Poshly*) He preferred be independent.

ONE (*Poshly*) He could cope perfectly well without help from anybody else. (*Neighbour exits*)

TWO Gently closing the car door, (*kicks it shut*)

ONE he set off to walk.

TWO Eventually,

ONE he arrived at the Health Centre.

TWO Tired!

ONE Breathless!

TWO (*Sternly*) And late!

ONE Tut! Tut!

TWO If only he'd called to his neighbour for help.

ONE He could have been saved the walk,

TWO and the repair bill,

ONE and being late.

TWO (*Obstinately*) But he could look after himself. (*Pause*)

ONE Next week Harry had to go to the Health Centre again.

TWO Not by bus.

ONE Not by car.

TWO He would go by train. After all the Health Centre was right by a station.

ONE Picking up his bag,

TWO he made tracks for the station.

ONE His train pulled in at the platform,

TWO and Harry opened the door . . .

ONE At least . . . he tried to open the door.

TWO But it was stuck.

ONE Would you believe it?

TWO No.

ONE Nor did Harry.

TWO So he put down his bag and pulled even harder.

ONE But the door was definitely,

TWO firmly,

ONE stuck! (*Guard enters*)

TWO Harry spotted a guard further down the platform,

ONE who could have sorted things out.

TWO (*Poshly*) But Harry preferred to be independent.

ONE (*Poshly*) He could cope perfectly well without help from anybody else.

TWO At that point the train began to move!!

ONE In a desperate bid, Harry threw his bag through a window and began to climb in after it!

TWO But then the guard spotted him,

ONE and pulled him back onto the platform,

TWO and issued a severe reprimand.

ONE Naughty boy! . . .

TWO he said angrily. (*Guard exits*)

ONE Steaming in annoyance,

TWO and feeling very small,

ONE Harry once again set off to walk.

TWO Eventually,

ONE he arrived at the Health Centre.

TWO Tired!

ONE Breathless!

TWO (*Sternly*) And late!

ONE Tut! Tut!

TWO If only he'd signalled to the guard for help.

ONE He could have been saved the walk,

TWO and a missing bag.

ONE and being late.

TWO (*Obstinately*) But he could look after himself.
(*Pause. Harry assumes sleeping position*)

ONE Next week,

TWO Harry woke up.

ONE He had decided to set off in good time and walk to the Health Centre.

TWO He looked at his watch.

ONE It was already eight o'clock!

TWO Oh, dear!

ONE He was already late!

TWO He lowered his feet to the floor,

ONE into a pool of water!

TWO Oh, no!

ONE He thought:

TWO Leaking . . . (*Harry looks at Narrator puzzled*) Sorry, leaping into action,

ONE He ran outside to check his roof.

TWO And noticed a large hole.

ONE Then he noticed several neighbours looking and laughing.

TWO He was still in his pyjamas.

ONE He moved swiftly into the house to make amends.

TWO Then,

ONE highly annoyed,

TWO and even more highly embarrassed,

ONE he seized his ladder,

TWO and placed it against the house.

ONE Only to find it was crooked.

TWO The house?

ONE No, just the ladder!

TWO Frustrated,

ONE Harry went inside and picked up the *Yellow Pages*,

TWO to phone for . . . (*Harry puts the* Yellow Pages *under his arm*) . . . Oh no . . . to place it under the ladder so that it wouldn't be crooked.

ONE He edged his way up the ladder,

TWO like an overweight hippopotamus,

ONE then on to the roof . . .

TWO and promptly fell off.

ONE Wheeeeeeeeeee . . .

TWO Bomp!

ONE Ouch!

TWO That hurt! (*Harry now on the ground, remains in this position to the end of the sketch*)

ONE Harry tried to get up,

TWO but didn't.

ONE Two hours later he was in hospital,

TWO badly injured.

ONE If only he'd admitted the job was beyond his capability.

TWO If only he'd called for someone who knew how to go about repairing a roof.

ONE   He would have been saved from such a nasty accident.

TWO   But he could look after himself? (*Harry, lying down, painfully nods to indicate that he still feels he can look after himself. Pause*)

ONE   Or could he?

WHERE ARE YOU?

A play by Mary Glover. Message follows in Epilogue.

Lady sitting on one side of the stage (representing one house) and a young girl sitting huddled up on stool or in some kind of box at the other side (representing another house)

PERSON   (*Picks up phone and dials*)

GIRL   (*Getting mobile phone from her pocket and speaking in a loud whisper*) Hello!

PERSON   Oh! Is that Jane?

GIRL   Yes!

PERSON   Is Daddy there, please?

GIRL   Yes, but he's very busy.

PERSON   Oh, well, can I speak to Mummy, please?

GIRL   She's very busy too.

PERSON   Is there anyone else there?

GIRL   Yes, the police are here.

PERSON   The police! Then can I speak to a police officer, please?

GIRL   No. They're very busy too!

PERSON Is there anyone else there who I CAN speak to?

GIRL   The Fire Brigade is here, but they are all VERY busy.

PERSON Jane! Whatever is going on? What are all those people doing there?

GIRL   Sh Shh – they are ALL looking for ME!

PERSON Looking for YOU? Well, where are you?

GIRL   I'm behind a big box at the back of the cupboard under the stairs. They looked in here but didn't see me!

PERSON Jane – listen! Mummy and Daddy and everyone else must be very worried as to where you have gone. So promise me you will get out of the cupboard NOW and let them know you are safe – and then let me speak to Daddy on the phone.

GIRL   All right then. I AM getting rather squashed and it's ever so dark in here. (*Pause, while she tries to get out. Whimpering*) I can't get this door open now. It's jammed or locked!

PERSON Keep banging on it and shouting "Mummy" as loud as you can!

GIRL   Mummy! Mummy! (*Bangs on floor and door*)

PEOPLE (*At the side of the stage*) Shhh! What's that? Listen! (*They rush towards the sound, open the door and embrace Jane and all ends happily.*)

EPILOGUE

Let us ask you now: Where are YOU? This little sketch was to illustrate Luke 19.10. "For the Son of Man came to seek and save what was lost". Are you disregarding him and doing your own thing, like Jane? Perhaps you are enjoying life, as she was at first, or maybe you have come to the point where it is not so much fun: it's rather boring and even frightening at times when you begin to realize everything around you is dark. If this is so, your only hope is to cry out to the Lord. You cannot save yourself. You are locked in with your sin. Jane's mother believed her daughter was lost or in danger somewhere – hence the police and fire brigade. She was ready to do anything in order to rescue her. Jesus sacrificed his life to save us because he loves us so much. Death could not hold him and he is alive for evermore. As soon as he hears our cry for help he will open the door to eternal life and real joy. He is our only hope!

CHAPTER TWELVE

A CHRISTMAS DRAMA

The People Who Miss Christmas, by Rhena Taylor

Cast: A narrator and two (versatile) actors.

Note that although a script is offered, this set of vignettes can be acted freely by inventive people without needing to learn lines. Just follow the idea.

NARRATOR introduces the production in some appropriate way, ending with: It's true we all know the Christmas story well, don't we? We hear it every year, many times over. But today we are going to think about those who, even though they were where it was all happening, still managed to miss Christmas entirely. Take King Herod for example:

VIGNETTE 1

READER Before Jesus was born in Bethlehem in Judea, during the time of King Herod, wise men from the east had set out to go to Jerusalem to seek the one who had been born King of the Jews. They had seen his star in the east and wanted to worship him.

NARRATOR   Herod's palace in Jerusalem. Herod and his wife. (*Some "kingly costume" a good idea. Herod sits gloomily on a chair . . . draped with some bright colour*)

WIFE   Morning, dear. You're not looking very bright today. What's the matter?

HEROD   Oh the usual things. I'm just fed up with being in this wretched country. Jews all over the place! Wanting this. Not wanting that. And now some weird old men are on the way here, following a star or some such nonsense. That's a joke if anything is! Stars all over the place if I had time to look at them. As if I didn't have enough to do!

WIFE   But what's it all about?

HEROD   I don't know and I don't care. I've got enough worries of my own.

NARRATOR   Herod missed Christmas. He was only thinking about his own troubles.

Bell

NARRATOR   Good Heavens Rest home. Anna visits her Dad. (*"Dad" old and grumbling. Glasses, foot up, etc.*)

ANNA   (*Brightly*) Here's your mail, Dad. And Susie made you some special biscuits. She's not very good at it yet, but she said it was for Christmas. I'm so sorry the Doctor feels you shouldn't come to us, but I promise, we'll come and visit you.

DAD   (*Sourly*) Christmas! Christmas! What's that to me? Stupid decorations that get in the way of the light, and rich food I can't eat.

ANNA   Come on, Dad. Make a little effort to join in with the others. It spoils it for them if you're sulking away here.

DAD   (*Angrily*) You'd sulk a bit if you were in my shoes. Living on slops, my arthritis giving me hell, and now they tell me my heart's playing up again. Then they come singing those wretched carols about peace and goodwill. Not much of that around here!

NARRATOR   Anna's Dad missed Christmas. He was only thinking about his own troubles.

(*Pause*)

READER   Lord, we pray at this Christmas time for those who are too worried to feel the joy of Christmas; too anxious, even angry, about their own situations to allow you to remind them that you love them. Draw near to them, Lord, with that love. Help them to feel deep within a sense of burdens being lifted, and enable them to give into your loving hands the concerns and anxieties they have. In Jesus name we ask it. Amen.

VIGNETTE 2

READER   Soon after Mary heard from the angel that she was to give birth to Jesus, she visited her cousin Elizabeth in the hill country of Judea. However, when the order came for Joseph and Mary to go to Bethlehem to take part in the census, there was no indication that the family came too.

NARRATOR   Zechariah and Elizabeth's home in the hill country of Judea. *(Zechariah (in an Israeli head-dress) is reading the law and Elizabeth is doing something domestic – with a broom, perhaps.)*

ELIZABETH   Zechariah, I can't help worrying about Mary! She shouldn't have been asked to go all the way to Bethlehem with the baby so near.

ZECHARIAH   Don't worry so much, Elizabeth. God will look after her and, you know, there will be quite a crowd of people going from here. They can help her.

ELIZABETH   But they won't be *family*! It's important when a baby is born to be all together. Perhaps we should have gone with them. The family should be together at a time like this! It's not right.

NARRATOR   Elizabeth missed Christmas. The family wasn't together.

Bell

NARRATOR   Mildred and Bill at the bus stop.

BILL   (*Smiling*) Hello Mildred! Getting colder, isn't it? All ready for Christmas, are you?

MILDRED   I don't know what you mean by that! Christmas to me means family time and I've got no one now since my Harold died and Andrew went off to America with my grandchildren.

BILL   Well, you've got a lot of friends at church, my dear! They're doing a Christmas lunch this year, I hear.

MILDRED   It's not the same. I feel Andrew *should* make the effort to visit me at Christmas time. After all, I am his mother! They've money enough to make the effort once a year!

NARRATOR   Mildred missed Christmas. The family wasn't together.

READER   Lord, we pray for families separated this Christmas: those too far to be able to visit one another and others split because of anger or disagreement. Let it be a time of reconciliation and love. And we pray for those many today who are without families, or who have known what it is to lose a loved partner or even a child. May they know the sense of the greater family of Christians and above all may they know you as Father and feel your love.

VIGNETTE 3

READER   And it came to pass in those days that there went out a decree from Caesar Augustus that all the world should be taxed. So Joseph went up from the town of Nazareth in Galilee to Judea, to Bethlehem with Mary, his espoused wife, being great with child. And so it was that, while they were there, the time came for the baby to be born and she gave birth to her firstborn, a son. She wrapped him in swaddling clothes and laid him in a manger; because there was no room for them in the inn.

NARRATOR   The Inn at Bethlehem. (*The innkeeper is wearing an apron and carrying bedding or any other household item. His wife comes in agog with news, eyes shining.*)

INNKEEPER For heaven's sake, Deborah, where have you been? The family in number 8 have been waiting for over an hour for this. (*He piles what he's carrying onto her*) Benjamin's in the kitchen but hasn't the faintest idea what to do about supper, and there are at least 20 people arriving within the hour who booked last year.

DEBORAH   (*Excited*) But . . . but there's something wonderful going on in the stable, Josiah! You know that couple we let go in there earlier. She's given birth.

INNKEEPER   May the Almighty bless her then! For heaven's sake. What's so wonderful about that? I'm telling you to . . .

DEBORAH   (*Interrupting*) No, no. It's not just that. Didn't you hear the men running in from the shepherd's field just now? They say there have been angels around in the sky, singing beautifully and telling the shepherds there that. . . .

INNKEEPER   (*Exasperated*) I tell you I've got enough to do without stories of angels. Sounds as if they've had too much to drink. *Will* you take that up to number 8 and then start telling Benjamin what to do in the kitchen . . .

NARRATOR   The innkeeper missed Christmas. He was just too busy.

Bell

NARRATOR   14 Harding Road. Haley and Jeff are getting ready for Christmas.

HALEY   (*Dumping down some supermarket bags on the floor*) Jeff, you really are the end! I told you not to get that bike for Rob. He's far too young for it. And it is *not* going on the top of the wardrobe. We haven't *got* a wardrobe, anyway. If you remember, we had fitted cupboards put in last month. Where have you been all morning, anyway? I thought I asked you to address those Christmas card envelopes. While you've been down to that bike centre, I've tired myself out at the supermarket. I've never seen such a rush. People seem to go mad at Christmas. And have you made up Auntie Gladys' bed like I told you to?

JEFF   (*Smiling at her*) It's OK. I can help you now. Look, the invitation to the church carol service has come. Let's try and go this year.

HALEY   (*Exasperated*) As if I've got time for that sort of thing!! Things are bad enough at Christmas without you getting all religious as well!

NARRATOR   Haley missed Christmas. She was just too busy.

READER   Lord, forgive us when we are too busy to make room for you in our lives. We see the rush of Christmas all around us: the need to shop and cook and write cards and decorate and go to many events. In it all, Lord, give us a heart at peace within – a willingness to give you time to speak to us, to read your word and remember that Christmas was the time when heaven broke into earth so that we might break into heaven.

VIGNETTE 4

READER   And there were in the same country shepherds abiding in the field, keeping watch over their flocks by night. And lo, the angel of the Lord appeared to them, and the glory of the Lord shone around them and they were sore afraid. And the angel said unto them: Fear not: for, behold, I bring you good tidings of great joy, which shall be to all people. For unto you is born this day in the city of David, a Saviour, which is Christ the Lord. And suddenly there was with the angel a multitude of the heavenly host praising God and saying: Glory to God in the highest and on earth peace, goodwill towards men. And it came to pass as the angels were gone away from them into heaven, the shepherds said one to another, Let us now go even unto Bethlehem, and see this thing which is come to pass. And they went with haste and found Mary and Joseph, and the babe lying in a manger.

NARRATOR   A field in Bethlehem. Enter two sheep.

SHEEP 1   Well! I like that! Straight off. Not a word to us. We could be eaten by wolves for all they care!

SHEEP 2   I quite agree. We should be their first priority. Angels or not!!

SHEEP 1   Those men need to get their priorities right! They're paid to be here, not somewhere else. Anyway, if they are off to see something special, why couldn't we go too? Leaving us behind like that! It's as if we don't matter!

NARRATOR	The sheep missed Christmas. They felt neglected, left out of things.

Bell

NARRATOR	Meals on wheels arrives at Joan's house.
TED	Here we are then, Joan. Happy Christmas! How are you today?
JOAN	(*Wrapped in a blanket*) Cold. That's what! Can't seem to get warm. Those old heaters don't give out anything.
TED	(*Cheerily*) I'll have a look at them in a minute. But let me get this Christmas dinner on a plate for you. Did you warm one for me? Here. I brought you a little present from Emma and me. She says she'll drop in on you later.
JOAN	Thanks very much! Not many people around to care about an old woman like me.
TED	Joan! You've got lots of friends around. You know you have.
JOAN	Yes, and what are they doing at Christmas? Looking after themselves. Proper left out, I am! Don't mean nothing to me, Christmas.
NARRATOR	Joan missed Christmas. She felt left out.
READER	Lord we pray for those who feel Christmas is passing them by: the lonely, the poor, the hungry, the refugee and the homeless. Lord, as help is sometimes offered at Christmas, may it be not only food and warmth, but also the message of the love of God in Jesus.

A brief talk can follow. The main point is: We can miss out on the glory of Christmas if we centre on ourselves. We don't miss out on anything if Christ is the centre of our day.

CHAPTER THIRTEEN

FOUR ASSORTED READINGS

THE VALLEY OF BACA

Blessed are those whose strength is in you, who have set their hearts on pilgrimage. As they pass through the Valley of Baca[1] they make it a place of springs; the autumn rains also cover it with pools.

Psalm 84.5–6

Whoever believes in me, as the Scripture has said, streams of living water will flow from within him.

John 7.38

We will be among the weak, the unlovely, the forgotten
in the valley of Baca

We will be with those whose capacity to love and be loved
    is fading away
in the valley of Baca

We will be with those whose bodies are weakening and
    pain is crippling
in the valley of Baca

We will be with those embittered by loss, angry at
    poverty, frightened of what lies ahead
in the valley of Baca

And we will make it a place of springs

The valley of weakness and neglect will become a garden
    of God's love
in the place of springs

Hopelessness and lovelessness will disappear as the
    green shoots of faith in God and the love of others begin
    to appear
in the place of springs

Weak bodies will house growing and joyful spirits and
    those in pain will feel God's arms about them
in the place of springs

Men and women will be made whole. Loss will be seen as
    gain and fear will fade in the knowledge that all life
    passes and the Kingdom of Heaven is yet to be entered
in the place of springs

Blessed indeed are those who pass through the Valley of
    Baca and make it a place of springs.

THE JERICHO ROAD

Reading: Luke 10.25–37.

The victim. It was a well known road – but he had to go down it. And he got into trouble.

Those who passed by also had to go along that road and saw the man lying there. They were afraid. They saw themselves reflected there. It could be me. They did not want to identify with the wretched body because their clothes were clean and they carried a lap-top computer. Their train was leaving soon. They doubted their ability to cope: after all, there are people who deal with things like that. Better leave it to them. They had had to sidestep too many already that week.

The one who stopped dealt well with the situation because it was just one man, and the donkey was able to carry him, and the inn had a room and needed business.

But that night he sat and thought. He had to go down that way again next Tuesday . . . and back on Wednesday. Supposing there were more people in need then?

In fact, there were three, one a woman who had fainted for lack of food. This time the inn was behind him, so he had to go back there before he could go on, and it really interfered with his timetable.

The price had gone up.

That's OK, said a friend when he got to Jericho. I've been meaning to start a business along there. I'll open another inn further down the road. Or we could have a string of bed and breakfast places.

Another friend started organizing a committee meeting. "You can collect money for this kind of thing," he said. "I'll do the promotion for you if you like."

People profit over brokenness.

The innkeeper wasn't nearly so friendly the following week when the traveller turned up with four more. "It's keeping proper people away having these people here. They use up the water, and their clothes are shabby and torn."

"Only because they have been abused and robbed," the traveller protested.

"Well, find another place. I don't want them here."

Next week the traveller decided he would "pass by" like the others – at least until the "charity" that his friend was organizing got going. It was too much. He had other business to attend to, and obviously his support team was letting him down.

He did that for a while, hurrying by looking the other way, but it didn't last. It gave him dreadfully guilty feelings. In the end he closed his business in Jericho and started to trade somewhere quite different. It was much more pleasant.

The Jericho road saw him no more.

TAKING THE ARMOUR OFF
Ephesians 6.13–17

He sat alone in his tent listening to the distant bustle and shouted orders that no longer seemed to concern him. The armour he had worn for so long seemed suddenly heavy, and piece by piece he began to take it off. In fact, it almost seemed as if there was someone else there helping him to do it.

First the belt of truth slipped to the floor. Truth. What was truth these days? Even the bishops didn't seem to agree about what they believed in. And as for the church – just a few people in it, the same faces day after day. Everyone else seemed to be getting on all right without God. Perhaps people were right. Truth was what you "wanted" to believe.

Then the breastplate of righteousness was carefully removed, and with that feelings of guilt overcame him. What good was he to the Master now? He couldn't do anything to stop the tide of evil and violence sweeping across the nation. He wasn't better than anyone else. Maybe it was presumptuous to say he was sure of going to heaven.

He shook off the strong leather shoes thankfully. He couldn't get out much these days anyway, and didn't see anyone to speak to about the "gospel of peace". In fact, when he thought about it, he hadn't mentioned his faith to anyone for months. When he did see the grandchildren they just weren't interested. "That's all old stuff," they'd said.

The shield of faith was already leaning against the wall of the tent. It was important in the days when he was at the forefront of the battle. But now? What use was it? No one was really bothering to attack him.

He looked with some sadness at the helmet: that bright and shining signal to all that he belonged to the Master, body and soul. He knew he did still, of course, but was that assurance still there? Was death really the gateway to heaven? Was Christ really waiting for him there? He looked away from the helmet and felt like crying.

Finally his sword lay beside him. He looked down at it. It at least was within reach, and he bent to pick it up. It had been through many a fight with him, and he fingered it lovingly. It was as sharp and bright as ever.

A darkness came upon the room. It felt as though someone or something near and evil was smiling, encouraging him to put it down again.

But he was accustomed to the sword and lifted it higher. It flashed suddenly in a ray of unexpected light.

Rejoice not against me O my enemy. For when I fall I shall arise . . .

Who had spoken? Why was the room suddenly free of evil? The sound of battle outside had drawn nearer. He could tell there was great pressure against his own side. Why was he not out there fighting?

He suddenly stood up. He seized the belt of truth and fastened it around his waist. He had known the truth of the gospel for many years. Why was he discarding it now? Against the breast of his own self-doubt and guilt he placed the breastplate of righteousness. This was his passport into the presence of God: the blood of the Saviour had made him righteous. Where were the shoes of the declaration of the gospel of peace? He hastily put them on, and with joy lifted once again the shield of faith. "For when I am weak, then am I strong"[2] . . . And the helmet. For a moment he put down the shield so he could lift that bright plumed helmet, the sign of his salvation in Jesus, and place it on his head. Then, taking up again the shield of faith, he picked up the sword: the word of God. He was ready, and he re-joined the fight.

AN EASTER BLESSING

They were walking in a great subdued crowd. The elderly woman was walking as fast as she could, anxious not to be left out. The walking stick was a great help, but her progress slowed. The others she was walking with began to overtake her, keeping up with the ones in front.

One man turned back and smiled sympathetically as he hurried by, concerned not to be left behind. A woman pushed by. "Don't worry about me," she said kindly. "I can get through."

They were arriving at their destination. The elderly woman was left behind, alone.

Did the people in the crowd even see the elderly woman as they hurried to be there on time? Did they care what happened to her as long as they didn't miss out? What was the situation? Were they hurrying for a train? Were they refugees, fleeing from danger?

No. Neither. This was the occasion of the Good Friday Walk of Christian Witness through the town centre. The people were all hurrying to keep up with the cross bearers. They were anxious not to miss being in time to present themselves at the cross before the servant king.

Were you there? Were you in the crowd who hurried by? Were you the woman who apologized as she pushed through, or the man who smiled but did not stop? The people on the Walk of Witness wanted to be the first to be close to their Lord for his blessing. But the Lord was not at the front of the crowd; he was not even at the coarse wooden cross held high at the front. He was bearing up his faithful old servant, giving her his arm, walking at her pace. She received the blessing.

Ruth Clinch
Used with permission.

CHAPTER FOURTEEN

GOOD HEAVENS

An evangelistic presentation with older people in mind,
by Rhena Taylor

The copyright of this dramatic production previously belonged to Outlook. We now release it to anyone who would like to make use of it. It is seen as evangelistic in nature (as against merely entertainment), and an invitation to commit (or re-commit) lives to Jesus Christ should be made at the end.

This basic script can be altered according to the team available and other Christian artists (who can contribute music/song/mime/dance) can fit their performances to the overriding themes as they appear. Check the script for accuracy. It has been used for a number of years and needs careful updating concerning space discoveries, world population figures, etc.

Timing: With the interval the show should take one and a half hours. (No longer!)

Minimum needs: Leader, Actors for "Bert and Annie", three good voices for Readers 1–3; one or two other readers (who can be there to dance, sing etc.). A music leader. As much as possible, all participants should be in the older age group.

Actuality participants (i.e. people being themselves): three members of the presenting team. Study where these come in the script. No testimony/interview should exceed four minutes.

Prelude: As people come in, perhaps for about fifteen minutes before the performance, there should be quiet but quite cheerful Christian music in the background, not vocal, perhaps a piano player or a tape mix. Ideally, those who are going to voice the script should not be present, but others should welcome the audience, help them get seated, etc.

Begins (on time!) with LEADER *and* READERS *on stage.* BERT *and* ANNIE *off stage to side. A welcome to the church may be given by the minister or another representative of the host church at this point, after which the leader speaks in general (i.e., not word for word!) as follows:*

LEADER   We would like to welcome you to this after-
         noon's presentation, which is brought to you by
         . . . . . ., which has as its main purpose the sharing
         of God's love shown us in Jesus, especially with
         those of the "third age". If, later, you'd like to
         know more about us, you will find . . . . . ., and
         we will be glad to answer questions. But just
         now we are those who have come to share the
         afternoon with you. I am . . . . . . from . . . . . ., and
         I'd like to introduce the team . . . (*Make it brief and*

use first names. Team smile, wave and say hello or equivalent.) Welcome again to Good Heavens, and we start by turning our thoughts away from earth: towards . . . well, towards what?

SFX   (*Weird, extra-terrestrial sound effects. Fade but stay in background.*)

READER 1 (*Declamatory*) What's out beyond the stars? Is it God?

READER 2 Our sun is the nearest star: 93 million miles away from us, eight hundred and seventy thousand miles in diameter; over a million times the size of earth.

READER 3 Our earth is a tiny planet, circling the sun. 70% of our surface is water. The rest of us live upon a crust lying on a core of molten and solid iron . . .

SFX out. Readers become more "relaxed" and open newspapers pretending to read (watch the crackle on the mike!) They sound excited. (Bring this up to date as needed.)

R1   October 12th 1998: A twenty billion pound international space station has been in the making for almost 14 years and is about to be assembled in space. It will sail around the earth at 18,000 miles an hour and be the size of two football pitches.

R2   Further analysis of the Cosmic Background Explorer satellite will shed light on the identity of the mysterious "dark matter" that we know contributes most of the mass of the universe.

R3   29th March 1996: There has been a breakthrough by British technology. We have received our clearest picture yet of the origins of the universe. The historic image of ripples in the radiation left by the creation of the universe is thought to be the "seeds" of galaxy clusters which formed out of the Big Bang fireball.

A distinctive sound (a bell or cymbal clash) to indicate that acting is taking place. It is sounded before and after the BERT and ANNIE scenes. In this script, it will be indicated by the word "Bell".

Bell

ANNIE *and* BERT. *They should be sitting but if difficult to see,* ANNIE *could be dusting and suddenly notices a newspaper, and picks it up.*

ANNIE   Bert! BERT! What do you make of all this stuff about galaxies and things in the sky? It says here we all started with a Big Bang. There's even a picture of it here. What do you really think's up there?

BERT   Up where?

ANNIE   Up in the sky! You know, they keep on about finding new things about it. How stars are made and that. They think there could be other worlds somewhere with people on them.

BERT (*Largely uninterested*) I could do with another world sometimes. One without kids in it for one. You seen what they've done to our fence again?

ANNIE If you didn't have kids, you wouldn't have people.

BERT What?

ANNIE Oh, never mind! It's just that sometimes I'd like to know more about what's really out there . . .

Bell

R1 What's out beyond the stars? Is it God?

R2 (*Begins as a usual prayer*) Our Father who art . . . (*Pause. More thoughtfully*) in heaven.

R3 (*Slowly. With emphasis*) In heaven.

R1 (*Thoughtfully*) I remember that one of the first Russian astronauts reported he didn't find God in outer space . . .

OVERHEAD 1 Rocket launch (*with SFX*)

R2 Did that Russian astronaut really think he would see you there, Lord? Did he think you were sitting way out there somewhere in a seeable form? Did he think he could sneak up and get a glimpse of you?

R3 Where is heaven, God? Out past even the farthest point in space that man will ever be able to probe? Or closer in . . . much closer . . . so close that it's really around us now – only we can't see it.

R1 It's just, I'd like to know . . .

LEADER   (*Suggested approach. Do not read*) Yes, we do ask questions like that: Where is God? What's out there anyway? Is there a God, and, if there is, why does he allow such awful things to happen? (*Refer to any recent accident, tragedy, natural disaster*) There was a man in the Bible who asked questions like that, called Job. Awful things happened to him: he lost all his possessions, his family died, he himself became very ill and he became very angry at God, asking, Why should I go on living when I have no hope? Why won't God answer my prayer? He throws me into a pit of filth and no one judges him! I'm tired of living! Why did he let me be born? He blocks my way and leaves me to die! Where is he? Why doesn't he answer? And God did answer . . . almost as if he finally "lost his temper" (if such a thing can happen to God) and the Bible says he answered Job "out of the storm".

A reading (selected) from Job 38. This should be "separated" from the other readers if possible, either by a totally different voice and place which cannot be seen by the audience or (preferably) by a recorded voice. During it, all on the "platform" are totally still. If a room can be darkened, appropriate slides can be shown during it.

RECORDING   Who is this that darkens my counsel with words without knowledge? Brace yourself . . . I will question you and you shall answer me.

Where were you when I laid the earth's foundation? Tell me, if you understand. Who marked off its dimensions? Who stretched a measuring line across it? On what were its footings set, or who laid its cornerstone – while the morning stars sang together and all the angels shouted for joy?

Who shut up the sea behind doors when it burst forth from the womb, when I made the clouds its garment and wrapped it in thick darkness?

Have you ever given orders to the morning, or shown the dawn its place?

Have you journeyed to the springs of the sea, or walked in the recesses of the deep?

Have the gates of death been shown to you?

What is the way to the abode of light? And where does darkness reside?

What is the way to the place where the lightning is dispersed, or the place where the east winds are scattered over the earth?

Who cuts a channel for the torrents of rain, and a path for the thunderstorm?

Can you bring forth the stars in their seasons?

Do you know the laws of the heavens?

Can *you* set up God's dominion over the earth?

LEADER (*Suggested*) When Job heard this, there wasn't much he could say. We read in the last chapter of the book of Job that he said: "I'm ashamed. I talked about things I didn't understand. I'm sorry."

Music break

Bell

BERT   All imagination, really, you know.

ANNIE   What is?

BERT   All that stuff about God. We'll never really know! It's like children making things up. You hear what young Emily did the other day?

ANNIE   No. What's that?

BERT   Made up some story about a whale in that gold-fish pond they have there.

ANNIE   A whale?

BERT   That's right. In that little pond they have in the garden. Wrote to that Greenpeace place about it and all! Len showed me the letters . . . laugh! Made my chest get bad again.

ANNIE   Well, Emily's always been one for letters. What did she say in them, anyway?

This extract, which is to lighten the show a little, should ideally be read by a child (or at least a young voice) and a friendly-voiced man. Drawn overheads (if an artist is around) can be used during it and credit for the story should be given either on an overhead or verbalized i.e.: This story is from the book *Dear Greenpeace* by Simon

James (1991: Walker Books, London). Permission was given to use the story in this way.

(*Note: the cast should listen appreciatively throughout and applaud at the end.*)

EMILY Dear Greenpeace, I love whales very much and I think I saw one in my pond today. Please send me some information on whales, as I think he might be hurt. Love, Emily.

GP Dear Emily, Here are some details about whales. I don't think you'll find it was a whale you saw, because whales don't live in ponds but in salt water. Yours sincerely, Greenpeace.

EMILY Dear Greenpeace, I am now putting salt into the pond every day before school and last night I saw my whale smile. I think he is feeling better. Do you think he might be lost? Love, Emily.

GP Dear Emily, Please don't put any more salt in the pond. I'm sure your parents won't be pleased. I'm afraid there can't be a whale in your pond because whales don't get lost. They always know where they are in the oceans. Yours sincerely, Greenpeace.

EMILY Dear Greenpeace, Tonight I am very happy because I saw my whale jump up and spurt lots of water. He looked blue. Does this mean he might be a blue whale? Love, Emily. PS What can I feed him with?

GP Dear Emily, Blue whales are blue and they eat

tiny shrimp-like creatures that live in the sea. However, I must tell you that a blue whale is much too big to live in your pond. Yours sincerely, Greenpeace. PS Perhaps it is a blue goldfish?

EMILY   Dear Greenpeace, Last night I read your letter to my whale. Afterwards he let me stroke his head. It was very exciting. I secretly took him some crunched-up cornflakes and breadcrumbs. This morning I looked in the pond and they were all gone! I think I shall call him Arthur. What do you think? Love, Emily.

GP   Dear Emily, I must point out to you quite forcibly now that in no way could a whale live in your pond. You may not know that whales are migratory, which means they travel great distances each day. I am sorry to disappoint you. Yours sincerely, Greenpeace.

EMILY   Dear Greenpeace, Tonight I'm a little sad. Arthur has gone. I think your letter made sense to him and he has decided to be migratory again. Love, Emily.

GP   Dear Emily, Please don't be too sad. It really was impossible for a whale to live in your pond. Perhaps when you are older you would like to sail the oceans studying and protecting whales with us. Yours sincerely, Greenpeace.

EMILY   Dear Greenpeace, It's been the happiest day! I went to the seaside and you'll never guess, but I saw Arthur! I called to him and he smiled. I knew it was Arthur because he let me stroke his head. I gave him some of my sandwich and then we said goodbye. I shouted that I love him very much and, I hope you don't mind, I said you loved him too. Love, Emily (and Arthur).

(*Applause*)

R1   But, is it "just imagination?" All this talk about God? Like a child playing games?

R2   Can we ever really know?

Bell

BERT   I suppose *somebody* did it.

ANNIE   Did what?

BERT   Made it. The world I mean. I wish I knew.

ANNIE   What's got into you? You weren't that interested a minute ago.

BERT   I know. It's just we're so small and there's such a lot of it out there. Do you think we really matter to anyone?

Bell

Actuality. The leader or another should give a short talk (three minutes) which is scripted below. Two questions basically are being answered at this point: (1) As Bert has just asked, Do we really matter to anyone? and (2) Can we ever really "know"? Can we be sure?

Suggested talk:

"That is a question we do ask from time to time: Can we possibly matter as individuals to anyone? The present world population is estimated at 6.2 billion (2001). Add to that those who have died or who are yet to be born, and they are numbers beyond our control. How could we really matter to anyone, even the Creator God?

"However, this never seemed a problem to God, who clearly knew all about numbers and said to Abraham (Genesis 22.17), 'I will surely bless you and make your descendants as numerous as the stars in the sky and as the sand on the seashore'. So God got it about right. He looked ahead without worrying. And Jesus was reassuring, too. He said: 'Are not two sparrows sold for a penny? Yet not one of them will fall to the ground apart from the will of your Father. And even the very hairs of your head are all numbered. So don't be afraid; you are worth more than many sparrows.' (Matthew 10.29–31). Almost as if he knew we'd ask that question!

"As for believing in God. It's quite hard not to (and polls tell us over 70% of people in the UK admit to believing in God) with the creation all around us! But when it comes to believing in Jesus, being a Christian, many people in England maybe don't believe it – or say they don't. But take heart. Over 32% of the world's population call themselves Christian. That's a lot of people. So don't throw it out without thinking a little. Because our country at this time mocks the Christian belief and because many of our churches seem to be empty, does not make eternity any the less true, nor does it change the mind of God.

"So, can we ever be 'sure'? No. How can we be? Our human minds will never grasp fully the secrets of the 'good heavens'. Christianity is a matter of faith.

"Jesus said: 'I tell you the truth. Whoever hears my word and believes him who sent me has eternal life.' (John 5.24), 'I am the resurrection and the life. He who believes in me will live, even though he dies.' (John 11.25).

"Is it so hard to believe? To trust God who made us? Does a child find it so hard when a parent says 'Don't touch the fire. It will hurt you. Don't run across that busy road'? Maybe the child doesn't understand, but he begins to trust the mother who said it. Is it so hard to trust God as we are here still children in his presence, as he says to us, 'Trust me, and one day you will grow up and really know what it means to live eternally in my presence.'?"

Music Break: A suggested hymn is "How Great Thou Art". Suitable background slides can be shown during the hymn if the room can be darkened.

R1	It's all right for some.
R2	They've got enough to live on.
R3	Got nice houses
R2	and a nice fat pension.
R3	Don't need to worry about the gas bill.
R2	Or taxes.
R3	Or the cracked pipe in the bathroom.
R1	It's all right for some.

R2   They keep warm in the winter

R3   and cool in summer.

R2   Never heard of arthritis

R3   or cataract operations.

R2   Or queueing at the post office on a Friday.

R3   Or getting off the bus in the market place.

R1   It's all right for some.

R2   But is it?

LEADER   Certainly life can get more difficult as we get older. We exist, in Outlook, especially to encourage "older people", but we have a really hard time discovering where they are. No one in our society wants to be called "old". When does old age begin, anyway?

R1   Old age begins just ten years ahead of my present age.

R2   Old age is when I bend down to tie my shoelaces and wonder what else I can do while I'm down there.

R3   Grey hair is a crown of splendour; it is attained by a righteous life.

R1   You're as old as you feel (and I feel about ninety!) (*Add here as inspiration dictates!*)

Audience participation. Leader can ask for other definitions from the audience.

LEADER   The story I've always liked is the one about the man of 93 who stepped on a rake by mistake and it nearly hit him in the face. "Cor," he said. "I could 'ave been blinded for life!" Yes, there's a lot to be said for the over 60s today.

R1 We were born before television, before peni-cillin, polio shots, frozen food, Xerox, plastic, contact lenses, videos, Frisbees and the Pill.

R2 We were before radar, credit cards, charge cards, split atoms, laser beams and ballpoint pens.

R3 Before dishwashers, microwaves, tumble driers, electric blankets, central heating, air condition-ers, drip-dry clothes . . .

R1 We got married first and then lived together (how quaint can you be?). We thought "fast food" was what you ate in Lent, a "big mac" was an oversized raincoat, a "joint" was what you had for Sunday lunch.

R2 We existed before house husbands, computer dating, instant coffee and disposable nappies, and when a "meaningful relationship" meant getting along with your cousins.

R3 We never heard of FM, tape decks, word proces-sors, artificial hearts, yoghurt or young men wearing earrings.

R1 We thought a "chip" was a piece of wood or a fried potato, a "mouse" was a four-legged animal, "grass" was mown, "coke" was what you kept in the coal house, "pot" was something you cooked in.

R2 Rock music was a fond mother's lullaby; a "gay" person was the life and soul of the party, "going all the way" meant staying on a double-decker to the bus depot, and "aids" meant a beauty treatment or help for someone in trouble.

R1   Yes, we who were born before 1946 must be a hardy bunch when you think of the way in which the world has changed and the adjustments we have had to make. No wonder we get confused sometimes.

R1   But by the grace of God . . .

R2   we have survived.

ALL R   Hallelujah!

Five minute stand-up-and-stretch interval.

Audience participation:

LEADER   (*Reminds the audience of the previous reading and says*) "Let's do this exercise the other way around!"

The leader selects a younger member of cast or a "plant" in the audience and sits them centre stage. The "game" then is for the audience to come up with words known by a majority of the audience (test by show of hands) which the younger person doesn't know. (E.g. "trilby", "flat irons" etc.). If more than half of the audience does know the meaning of the words and the younger person doesn't, the proposer in the audience gets a "prize". Take it lightly, maybe three or four times.

LEADER   Yes, there is a generation gap around, but in the end it doesn't really matter what age we are. We're all in the same boat, trying to understand what it means to be a human being on this small sphere we call earth, what we should be doing, what our responsibilities are; and within all of us, somewhere, is a human spirit looking out and up, with that hunger for something beyond ourselves, beyond this earth. We search for God and call ourselves Christians.

(*Note: In the first performances of this, we used a dancer here, who showed in her dance the search of the human spirit for Christ*)

Bell

BERT   (*A magazine in his hand*) Annie, what about being atheists?

ANNIE   Being what?

BERT   Atheists. People who don't believe God exists. There's an article here that says we're (*consults the magazine*) an "inextricable multiplicity of ascending and descending life-processes". By someone called Nietzsche (or something like that).

ANNIE   You on about that universe business again?

BERT   I suppose so. I've been reading this article about someone who's an atheist.

ANNIE   But we can't be that. We're Christians!

BERT   Are we?

ANNIE   Well, yes. I think so anyway. We go to church . . . sometimes.

BERT   Last Christmas.
ANNIE   Well, what do you have to do to be a Christian
         anyway?

Bell

Actuality: (*A team member can speak here.*) What does being
a Christian mean to her/him? What did she think was a
Christian and when did she find out what it really was?
This is partly a personal testimony but also the first
mention of what it means to be a real Christian. (Answer
should cover the fact that people "think they're all right"
if they live a good life and go to church occasionally.) The
person can lead into her favourite hymn. In the first performances, the speaker led into "For the joys and for the
sorrows . . . For this we have Jesus".

Music break

Bell

BERT   Got to tell you something, Annie.
ANNIE   What's that?
BERT   All this talk about Jesus, the bit about "knowing
         him". Seems a bit "personal" somehow. Makes
         me embarrassed.
ANNIE   I know what you mean. I've heard people talk
         about Jesus too. You know, Bert, the trouble is,
         you and me, we've never really thought about
         God like that. He belongs in church, not here in
         our home.

BERT   Yes. The way some people talk you'd think he was around all the time – kind of helping us people out.

ANNIE   (*Wistfully*) I'd love to know him like that. Things would be so different! Just supposing it was true!

Bell

READING (Supposing it was true. Background music.)

R1   Because God has come in Jesus, then everything can be different.

R2   We can be different, each one of us.

R3   We can be remade, remoulded, renewed. No longer alone.

R1   Supposing we could be like that. Supposing it was true!

R2   We could walk through this changing perplexing world with a peace in our hearts that nothing could take away.

R3   We could bear the suffering and darkness around us, and still recognize the pity and compassion of God.

R1   Supposing we could be like that. Supposing it could be true!

R2   We could give our family and our friends into the hands of God, knowing he loves them even more than we do.

R3   We could lose the bitterness of hurtful memories, be free of the guilt within us.

R1   Supposing we could be like that. Supposing it
            could be true.

R2   We could lose our fear of the future: fear of
            illness, fear of death.

R3   We could learn to really trust in God, through
            everything. It would make such a difference in
            our lives.

R1   Supposing we could be like that. Supposing it
            could be true.

(*Background music fade out*)

LEADER   Yes, just suppose . . . ! We believe in Jesus but can
            he really change our lives like that?

Actuality. Interview or straight testimony from an
Outlook member who hasn't had life easy, but did find
his/her life change with Jesus.

Music break: A suggestion is "Knowing you" . . .

LEADER   Yes, it's a lovely song, isn't it? But what exactly
            do we need to "know" about Jesus to find that
            he becomes a real part of our daily lives? (*Leader
            should here give a brief but clear answer to the ques-
            tion of what "knowing Jesus" actually means. The
            equivalent of the "four spiritual laws"! Keep it short
            and lead into the reading that follows:*)

R1   (*Steadily*) For God so loved the world

R2   (*Excited*) All of us. Not just the ones in Christian countries. Not just the ones who try to be good. Who call on his name. Everyone!

R1   . . . that he gave his one and only son

R3   Jesus. He's called the Prince of Peace, God's Beloved Son, Emmanuel, the Great High Priest, the Holy One of God, the Morning Star, the Sun of Righteousness, the Saviour of the World.

R1   That whoever believes in him

R2   Anywhere! Everywhere! At any time and place we can say, Here I am, Lord. I believe! Take my life.

R1   Shall not perish

R3   I've been afraid of that, Lord. Afraid of dying. Getting lost, going somewhere strange, never seeing anyone again. So I'm glad, so glad I will not perish, Lord.

R1   But have eternal life.

R2   Tell me about it, Lord.

BERT and ANNIE (*Who do not appear again*, can read these perhaps with a brief word of testimony)

BERT   "Then I saw a new heaven and a new earth, for the first heaven and the first earth had passed away, and there was no longer any sea. I saw the Holy City, the new Jerusalem, coming down out of heaven from God, prepared as a bride beautifully dressed for her husband. And I heard a loud voice from the throne saying, 'Now the dwelling of God is with men, and he will live with them. They will be his people, and God himself will be with them and be their God. He will wipe every tear from their eyes. There will be no more death or mourning or crying or pain, for the old order of things has passed away.' He who was seated on the throne said, "'I am making everything new.'" (Revelation 21.1–5a)

ANNIE   "Then I looked and heard the voice of many angels, numbering thousands upon thousands, and ten thousand times ten thousand. They encircled the throne and the living creatures and the elders. In a loud voice they sang: 'Worthy is the Lamb, who was slain, to receive power and wealth and wisdom and strength and honour and glory and praise!'

"Then I heard every creature in heaven and on earth and under the earth and on the seas, and all that is in them singing: 'To him who sits on the throne and to the Lamb, be praise and honour and glory and power, for ever and ever!'" (Revelation 5.11–13)

LEADER   This presentation is called "Good Heavens". We began with man looking out, trying in his own strength and vision to understand some of the secrets of the universe. We end with looking at what God has told us about it.The Bible says *No eye has seen, no ear has heard, no mind has conceived what God has prepared for those who love him but God has revealed it to us by his Spirit* . . . 1 Corinthians 2.9. Yes, there's a lot ahead. And as we get older we get nearer to it. But we still have this life to live. What about now? We are not Christians only to get into heaven(!) but to enjoy the Lord's presence in our day to day life.

Actuality. A testimony (perhaps by an older person who isn't finding his/her situation all that comfortable) "Living with Jesus day by day." This is a good time to make some mention of the need for prayer and Bible reading . . .

Music break

The ending As the Spirit leads and according to what we are actually asking the members of the audience to do (i.e., are cards of decision – or re-committal – available? What follow-up mechanism is in place?) A final hymn can be sung.

In the first performances we listened to "Only by grace". Then the leader explained why the presentation had taken place. Something like: This is not just entertainment. We have something real to say. All of us are reaching old age and it could be tough going. Don't try it without Jesus. There was then an appeal, a prayer, and explanation of the commitment cards used, and a statement that none of us were rushing away. We were around for prayer and chatting over tea. We ended singing "There is a Redeemer".

CHAPTER FIFTEEN

AND FINALLY . . .

"What do you really want out of life?" the interviewer asked a famous footballer who had just pulled off a contract worth millions. "I suppose . . ." he said, and paused. "I suppose to be happy."

I think he had it right.

It is a strange new world today that we live in, so different from the one we once knew. The rate of change is accelerating ever faster, not only on one level but simultaneously on many. Computers are our masters, and the Worldwide Web seems to make the world shrink to the size of a village that we no longer feel we inhabit.

But maybe it doesn't greatly matter whether we need to discuss the performance of the latest 1,200 MHz computer processor with a Japanese businessman over the Internet, or chat to an older person sitting on a bench looking out over the sea; whether we send a weekly e-mail to our daughter 4,000 miles away or talk to our neighbour as we queue up in the post office. The important thing is to communicate – to find love and friendship around us, to laugh with our friends and family, to share special moments together. This is to be part of the human race.

I wonder why Jesus chose to be one of the "ordinary" people. "Where did this man get these words from?" asked the people of Nazareth. "Isn't this the carpenter's son?" (Matthew 13.55). Jesus spent his childhood in a small and unimportant town in occupied territory. He chose the job of an artisan. He rode a donkey (a small Fiat?) rather than a six-horse chariot to enter Jerusalem. I wonder what would have happened if the Father God had sent him to earth when every television screen in the world might have briefly focused on him and his miracles? Maybe we would have missed out on his message altogether.

Yes, the world is caught in the turbulent waves of change. Perhaps in the centuries to come, a sort of "Star-Trek" life will be a real possibility. The opening up of extra-terrestrial exploration is thrilling, exciting and something that will never stop because God has given us that enquiring and restless mind. Thank him for it. We are made in his image. He, the Creator, has passed on that creativity to mankind, and it can be used for good or evil.

This is the human being God has created, and it will remain so until God says "enough is enough". Then the race on earth will stop, for we will be in the presence of the Creator of it all. Whatever happens then, the Christian will be at peace, for "No eye has seen, no ear has heard, no mind has conceived what God has prepared for those

who love him, but God has revealed it to us by his Spirit."
(1 Corinthians 2.9–10)

Notice those last words. It may be that the vision of that
future in the eyes and mind of an older saint may leave
the wonders of earth far behind.

APPENDIX

BASIC STATISTICS ON AGEING

The United Kingdom

An Ageing Population

In 1999, the population of the United Kingdom based on mid-year estimates was 59,501,000. Of this figure, 18% were over pensionable age:

- 6,908,000 were women aged 60 and over (of whom 5,448,000 were aged 65 and over)
- 3,845,000 were men aged 65 and over
- 9,293,000 were people aged 65 and over
- 4,364,000 were people aged 75 and over
- 1,142,000 were people aged 85 and over.[1]

In 1997 a man of 60 could expect to live for another 18.8 years and a woman of the same age for 22.6 years.[2]

In 1996, in England and Wales, 5,523 people (4,943 women and 580 men) were aged 100 and over. In 2036 there will be an estimated 39,000 people in this age group.[3]

An Ageing Population in the Future

The number of people over pensionable age, taking account of the change in the women's retirement age, is projected to increase from 10.7 million in 1998 to 11.9 million in 2011, and will rise to 12.2 million by 2021.[4]

Income

(GB) In February 1999, 1,620,000 people aged 60 or over (single people or couples) were receiving Income Support (Minimum Income Guarantee) because of their low income.[5]

The Department of Social Security estimates that in 1997/98 between 27% and 37% of pensioners who were entitled to Income Support, between 0% and 12% who were entitled to Housing Benefit, and between 20% and 31% entitled to Council Tax Benefit, did not claim.[6]

Living Alone

(GB) In 1998, in the 65–74 age group, 19% of men and 34% of women lived alone, and 29% of men and 59% of women aged 75 and over lived alone.[7]

(GB) In 1998, the likelihood of living alone increased with age, from 19% of men and 31% of women aged 65–69, to 43% of men and 72% of women aged 85 and over. "Older" elderly people were more likely to be living with a son or daughter, rising from 4% of those aged 65–69, to 8% of those aged 85 and over.[8]

Leisure, Learning and Computers

In May 2000, 4 million people aged over 50 owned a computer, spending an average of 9 hours per week using it.[9]

In 1997, in England and Wales, 55% of women and 27% of men aged 60–69 took part in some sort of learning for leisure purposes.[10]

(GB) In 1996–7, walking was the most popular physical activity for older people, with 49% of men and 41% of women aged 60–69, 34% of men and 25% of women aged 70–79, and 19% of men 9% of women aged 80 and over, engaging in a walk of two miles or over in the four weeks before interview.[11]

The Safety and Health of Older People

(GB) In 1998, it was estimated that some 5% of the population aged 65 and over, and 20% of the population aged 80 and over, suffered from dementia.[12]

In 1998, in England and Wales, the deaths of 178 people aged 65 and over involved hypothermia as the underlying cause according to their death certificates.[13]

In 1998, nearly 17% of all accidents within the home involved people of 65 and over.[14]

(GB) In 1998, of 906 pedestrian fatalities on the road, 422 (47%) were over the age of 60.[15]

Housing

In 1996, in England, 18.7% of single older people (over 60) lived in poor housing. Of people aged 75 and over, 19.9%

of households lived in poor housing. The homes of 365,000 (12%) older lone persons (over 60) required essential modernization, compared to a figure of 6% for all households.[16]

(GB) In 1998, 4% of people aged 65–69, 7% of people aged 70–74, 11% of people aged 75–79, 17% of people aged 80–84 and 20% of people aged 85 and over lived in sheltered accommodation.[17]

Sources of UK Data Used

1. *Population Trends* (PT) 101, Autumn 2000, table 1.5 (Population: age and sex) and table 1.2 (Population national).
2. Ibid., table 1.5 (Expectation of life [in years] at birth and selected age).
3. "The demography of centenarians in England and Wales". *PT*, 96, Summer 1999, © Crown Copyright 1999, annex 1.
4. *National population projections: 1998–based*, National Statistics, © Crown Copyright 2000, table 3.2 (Actual and projected population by age, UK, 1998–2021).
5. *Social Security statistics 1999*, Department of Social Security, 1999, table A2.05 (Income support recipients by type of recipient).
6. *Income related benefits – estimates of take up in 1996/97 (revised) and 1997/98*, Department of Social Security, 1999, tables 1.1, 2.1 and 3.1.
7. Living in Britain: results from the 1998 General

Household Survey (GHS), Office for National Statistics, © Crown Copyright 2000, table 3.14 (percentage living alone, by age and sex).

8. *People aged 65 and over . . . an independent study carried out . . . as part of the 1998 General Household Survey* (PA65O), Office for National Statistics, © Crown Copyright 2000, section 2: characteristics of people aged 65 and over.

9. *Older people and IT fact card*, Age Concern England, 2000.

10. Social focus on older people, op cit., table 2.11 (Types of taught learning: by gender and age, 1997).

11. Ibid., table 2.14 (Participation in the most popular sports, games and physical activities: by gender and age, 1996–7).

12. "Dementia in people aged 65 years and older: a growing problem?" *Population Trends* 92, Summer 1998, © Crown Copyright 1998.

13. *1998 mortality statistics: cause, England and Wales*, Office for National Statistics, © Crown Copyright 1999, table 2 (Deaths: underlying cause, sex and broad age-group, 1998).

14. *Home accident surveillance system including leisure activities, 1998 data, 22nd annual report*, Department of Trade and Industry, 2000, table HASS 4 (Location of accident within the home by age).

15. *Road accidents Great Britain 1998: the casualty report*, Department of Environment, Transport and the Regions, 1999, table 33 (Casualties: by age, road user type and severity: 1998).

16. *English house condition survey 1996,* Department of Environment, Transport and the Regions, 1998, chapter 7.
17. PA65O, op cit., table 7 (People living in sheltered accommodation by age and household type).

Europe

Population growth fastest among the "very old"

Between 1960 and the present day, the proportion of older people (65 years and over) in the population has risen from 11% to 16%. All the signs are that this trend will continue well into the century. By 2010, there will be twice as many older persons (69 million) as in 1960 (34 million).

About 45% of the "very old" live alone

The majority of the European Union's elderly population (aged 65 and over) live either alone (32%) or with their partner (51%). A further 13% live with their children (or other relatives/friends). Only 4% live in a home or institution. It is clear, however, that demand for housing and care changes considerably as people grow older.

(*Source: The social situation in the European Union 2000, Eurostat.*)

Australia

The Older Population

At 30 June 1998 there were 2.3 million older people (those aged 65 and over) in Australia. The older population is increasing – both in number and as a proportion of the total population – each year. Whereas older people comprised 12% of the total population in 1998, they are projected to form almost one-quarter (24%) of the total population by 2051.

(*Source: Australian Bureau of Statistics*)

United States

The Older Population

The older population – persons 65 years or older – numbered 34.5 million in 1999. They represented 12.7% of the U.S. population, about one in every eight Americans. The number of older Americans increased by 3.3 million or 10.6% since 1990, compared to an increase of 9.1% for the under-65 population.

Since 1900, the percentage of Americans 65 or older has more than tripled (4.1% in 1900 to 12.7% in 1999), and the number has increased eleven times (from 3.1 million to 34.5 million).

The older population itself is getting older. In 1999 the 65–74 age group (18.2 million) was eight times larger than in 1900, but the 75–84 group (12.1 million) was 16 times larger and the 85+ group (4.2 million) was 34 times larger.

(*Source: Compiled primarily from Internet releases of the U.S. Bureau of the Census and the National Center for Health Statistics*)

Future Growth

By 2030, there will be about 70 million older persons, more than twice their number in 1999. People 65+

represented almost 13% of the population in the year 2000 but are expected to grow to be 20% of the population by 2030.

(Source: A Profile of Older Americans: 2000, Administration on Aging, U.S. Dept. of Health and Human Services)

Our ageing world

One of the major achievements of the twentieth century was an increase in life expectancy in almost every country in the world. At the same time fewer children are being born as people become more able to plan their families. These two factors mean that across the world populations are getting older, with a high number of older people and a smaller proportion of younger people. This population change is happening fastest in less-developed countries.

An ageing world is a female world

Nearly everywhere, women outlive men. At 60 years old there are 99 males to every 100 females. At the age of 80 and over, there are just 69 males to every 100 females.

Women often outlive their spouses, meaning they are more likely to be living alone in old age. In many countries of Africa and Asia, more than half of all women aged 60 and over are widowed, compared to 10–20% of men. Women are also less likely than men to remarry if their spouse has died.

The oldest old

In many countries of the world the oldest old (75 years and over) are the fastest growing portion of the older population.

A few interesting church statistics

- The percentage of English churchgoers who were 65 or over in:
  - 1979 was 18%,
  - 1989 19%, and in
  - 1998 25%
- In 1979 there were 600,000 people in their 60s who attended church. By 1989 this number had reduced to 400,000, and by 1998 to 270,000.
- In 1979 there were 430,000 people in their 70s attending church. By 1989 these had been reduced to 250,000 in their 80s, and by 1998 to 20,000 in their 90s.
- There were 220,000 people aged 80 or over attending church in 1979.

NOTES

Prologue

1. Help the Aged Information sheet. April 2000
2. Brierley, Peter, *Turning the Tide*, London: Christian Research, 2000 (p. 117, table 31)
3. English house condition survey 1996, *DETR* 1998, chapter 7
4. Help the Aged, *The Older Population*, April 2000, p. 10
5. Help the Aged, *op. cit.*, p. 13

Chapter One: Starting Out

1. Brierley, Peter, *op. cit.*
2. English Church Attendance Survey, Christian Research, 1994

Chapter Four: The Church and Its Older Members

1. Christian Vocations (01384 233511)
2. Senior Volunteer Network (01623 793863)

Chapter Six: Waking Up the Wednesday Afternoon Fellowship

1. *Born to Shop*, Mike Starkey (Monarch, Eastbourne, p. 27)
2. *The Country of Old Age*, Shirley Toulson (Hodder & Stoughton: London, 1998)

Chapter Seven: A "Holiday at Home"

1. Christian Publicity Organisation, Garcia Estate, Canterbury Road, Worthing, W. Sussex BN13 1BW, UK (01903 264556; e-mail: cpo@pavilion.co.uk)

Chapter Nine: Lots of Lovely Ideas

1. "Evangelism" June 2000.

Chapter Thirteen: Four Assorted Readings

1. Hebrew: Weeping
2. 2 Corinthians 12.10